RETIREMENT ISSUES, PLANS AND LIFESTYLES



# THE ROLE OF SAVINGS AND OTHER ISSUES IN RETIREMENT READINESS

# RETIREMENT ISSUES, PLANS AND LIFESTYLES

Additional books in this series can be found on Nova's website at:

https://www.novapublishers.com/catalog/index.php?cPath=23_29&seriesp=
Retirement+Issues%2C+
Plans+and+Lifestyles

Additional e-books in this series can be found on Nova's website at:

https://www.novapublishers.com/catalog/index.php?cPath=23_29&seriespe=
Retirement+Issues%2C+Plans+and+Lifestyles

RETIREMENT ISSUES, PLANS AND LIFESTYLES

# THE ROLE OF SAVINGS AND OTHER ISSUES IN RETIREMENT READINESS


JOEL K. HARRIS
EDITOR



Nova Science Publishers, Inc.
*New York*

**NOTICE TO THE READER**



**Library of Congress Cataloging-in-Publication Data**
The role of savings and other issues in retirement readiness / editor, Joel K. Harris.
p. cm.
Includes index.
ISBN 978-1-60741-446-9 (hardcover)
1. Retirement--Economic aspects--United States. 2. Retirement income--United States. 3. Retirement--United States--Planning. 4. Social security--United States. 5. Pensions--Economic aspects--United States. I. Harris, Joel K.
HQ1062.R65 2010
332.024'014--dc22

*Published by Nova Science Publishers, Inc. ✦ New York*

# CONTENTS

# PREFACE

The 78 million members of the "baby boom" generation are beginning to retire. After many years of accumulating assets to spend in retirement, they now must decide how to convert these assets into a steady stream of income. Since the trend has shifted from defined benefit pensions to defined contribution plans such as 401(k) plans, future retirees will be less likely to have a guaranteed stream of income from defined benefit pensions. While Social Security will provide a guaranteed income to most retirees, it will replace only a relatively small proportion of their pre-retirement income. As a result of these trends, many future retirees will rely greatly on their savings to finance their consumption during retirement. This book examines the role of savings and other related issues in retirement readiness.

Chapter 1 - Most Social Security beneficiaries pay Medicare premiums. Unless they qualify for low-income assistance, beneficiaries who participate in Medicare Part B (Supplementary Medical Insurance) or Part D (prescription drugs) must pay monthly premiums to receive coverage. Part B participants have premiums automatically deducted from their Social Security benefit checks. Starting in 2007, higher-income Part B beneficiaries must pay higher Part B premiums. An estimated 5% of Part B beneficiaries must pay income-related premiums in 2008. Part D participants may choose to have their premiums deducted from their Social Security checks. The amount of Part D premiums varies widely by plan. Beneficiaries must also pay other out-of-pocket costs when they use Part B and Part D services.

Medicare premiums are absorbing a growing share of Social Security benefits. To see the effect of growing premiums, consider a Social Security beneficiary who earned the average wage throughout his or her career (called a *medium earner*). If this retiree chose to participate in Part B — as the vast majority of Social Security beneficiaries do — the standard Part B premium would have absorbed about 5% of the retiree's benefits in 1999 and about 8% in 2008. The proportion of benefits needed to pay the standard Part B premium rose by almost 50% over the past decade.

The introduction of Medicare Part D adds to the premium expenses of beneficiaries who choose to participate; it also substantially reduces their out-of-pocket prescription drug costs. Part D premiums vary widely among plans; this chapter focuses on average premiums for standard coverage plans. If a medium earner chose to participate in both Part B and Part D, about 11% of his or her Social Security benefits would be used for combined Parts B and D premiums in 2008.

Medicare's trustees project that premiums for Parts B and D will grow at a faster rate than Social Security benefits in the future, thus consuming a greater proportion of benefits over time. By 2080, the Medicare trustees project that as a proportion of Social Security benefits, premiums will more than double. In 2080, a medium earner is projected to need 15% of his or her benefits to pay the Part B premium and 23% of his or her benefits to pay combined Parts B and D premiums.

The deduction of Medicare premiums affects beneficiaries differently, depending on their incomes and Social Security benefit amounts. Medicare premiums absorb a greater fraction of lower earners' Social Security benefits than of higher earners' benefits, because benefit amounts are progressive. However, some low-income beneficiaries are eligible for subsidies that cover their Medicare premiums and other out-of-pocket costs. Other beneficiaries with low benefits may be protected by a hold harmless provision that prevents a beneficiary's Social Security check from declining because of increases in the standard Part B premium.

Finally, it is important to note that although Social Security beneficiaries are affected by rising health-care costs, the benefits of participating in Medicare are substantially greater than the costs.

Chapter 2 - Several types of savings are eligible for beneficial treatment under the individual income tax, and Individual Retirement Accounts (IRAs) have received considerable attention. Pension savings are actually more important in terms of revenue loss. There are other investments that are treated favorably as well. The President has proposed in a succession of budgets to significantly expand IRAs. Effects of these provisions on savings are uncertain, and, despite dollar limits on contributions and income phase outs, IRAs tend to benefit higher income individuals.

Chapter 3 - Older Americans are an economically diverse group. In 2007, the median income of individuals aged 65 and older was $17,382 but incomes varied widely around this average. One-fourth of Americans 65 or older had incomes of less than $10,722 in 2007, while another one-fourth had incomes of $32,160 or more. As Congress considers reforms to Social Security and the laws governing pensions and retirement savings plans, it may be helpful to examine how changes to one income source would affect each of the others, and thus the total income of older Americans.

Older persons receive income from a variety of sources, including earnings, pensions, personal savings, and public programs such as Social Security and Supplemental Security Income. Using data from the March 2008 *Current Population Survey*, this chapter describes the number of elderly individuals and households receiving income from each of these sources and the distribution of income across individuals and households.

Retirement benefits from Social Security and pensions are the most common sources of income among the aged. In 2007, Social Security paid benefits to 86% of individuals aged 65 and older and to 89% of households in which the householder or the householder's spouse was 65 or older. Social Security is also the largest single source of income among the aged. Sixty-nine percent of Social Security beneficiaries aged 65 or older received more than half of their income from Social Security in 2007. For 41% of elderly recipients and 29% of elderly households, Social Security accounted for more than 90% of total income in 2007. One-third of people aged 65 and older, and fewer than one-half of elderly households, received income from a private or public pension in 2007. Among individuals aged 65 or older who reported income from a government pension, median pension income was $16,629. Among recipients of private pensions, the median pension received in 2007 was just $7,200.

Many Americans prepare for retirement by saving and investing some of their income while they are working. Of the 36.8 million Americans aged 65 and older who were living in households in 2007, 18.9 million (5 1%) received income from assets, such as interest, dividends, rent, and royalties. Most received small amounts of income from the assets they owned. Of individuals aged 65 or older who received income from assets in 2007, half received less than $1,585. Of households with a householder or spouse aged 65 or older, 57% percent received income from assets in 2007. Among these households, median income from assets in 2007 was $2,254.

Earnings are an important source of income for older Americans, especially those under age 70. Although there was a trend toward earlier retirement from about 1960 to 1985, over the past 20 years more Americans have continued to work at older ages. In 2007, median earnings of individuals aged 55 to 64 who worked were $37,000, while the median earnings of workers aged 65 to 69 were $25,000. Among all workers 65 and older, median earnings in 2007 were $20,000. Poverty among those aged 65 and older has fallen from one in three older persons in 1960 to less than one in ten today. Although the overall rate of poverty is relatively low, it remains high for women, minorities, the less-educated, and people over age 80.

Chapter 4 - To a worker contemplating retirement, there is perhaps no more important question than "How long will my money last?" Congress has a strong interest in the income security of older Americans because much of their income is either provided directly from public programs like Social Security, or in the case of pensions and retirement accounts, is subsidized through tax deductions and deferrals.

Many retirees must decide how to convert retirement account balances into income and how to preserve the accounts in the face of several kinds of risk.

Chapter 5 - In the interest of encouraging workers to save for retirement, Congress has authorized several kinds of retirement savings plans that qualify for reduced or deferred income taxes. These plans provide a financial incentive for people to save, either by allowing workers and employers to deduct from income the amount they contribute to the plan or to take tax-free distributions from the plan after they retire. This CRS report summarizes the provisions of law that govern the taxes applicable to pre-retirement distributions from retirement accounts, and the situations in which distributions must be taken from a plan in order to avoid a tax penalty.

Chapter 6 features testimony before the U. S. House of Representatives.

In: The Role of Savings and Other Issues… ISBN: 978-1-60741-446-9
Editor: Joel K. Harris 

*Chapter 1*

# THE IMPACT OF MEDICARE PREMIUMS ON SOCIAL SECURITY BENEFICIARIES*

*Kathleen Romig*

## SUMMARY

Most Social Security beneficiaries pay Medicare premiums. Unless they qualify for low-income assistance, beneficiaries who participate in Medicare Part B (Supplementary Medical Insurance) or Part D (prescription drugs) must pay monthly premiums to receive coverage. Part B participants have premiums automatically deducted from their Social Security benefit checks. Starting in 2007, higher-income Part B beneficiaries must pay higher Part B premiums. An estimated 5% of Part B beneficiaries must pay income-related premiums in 2008. Part D participants may choose to have their premiums deducted from their Social Security checks. The amount of Part D premiums varies widely by plan. Beneficiaries must also pay other out-of-pocket costs when they use Part B and Part D services.

Medicare premiums are absorbing a growing share of Social Security benefits. To see the effect of growing premiums, consider a Social Security beneficiary who earned the average wage throughout his or her career (called a

* This is an edited, reformatted and augmented version of a CRS Report for Congress publication dated January 2008.

*medium earner*). If this retiree chose to participate in Part B — as the vast majority of Social Security beneficiaries do — the standard Part B premium would have absorbed about 5% of the retiree's benefits in 1999 and about 8% in 2008. The proportion of benefits needed to pay the standard Part B premium rose by almost 50% over the past decade.

The introduction of Medicare Part D adds to the premium expenses of beneficiaries who choose to participate; it also substantially reduces their out-of- pocket prescription drug costs. Part D premiums vary widely among plans; this chapter focuses on average premiums for standard coverage plans. If a medium earner chose to participate in both Part B and Part D, about 11% of his or her Social Security benefits would be used for combined Parts B and D premiums in 2008.

Medicare's trustees project that premiums for Parts B and D will grow at a faster rate than Social Security benefits in the future, thus consuming a greater proportion of benefits over time. By 2080, the Medicare trustees project that as a proportion of Social Security benefits, premiums will more than double. In 2080, a medium earner is projected to need 15% of his or her benefits to pay the Part B premium and 23% of his or her benefits to pay combined Parts B and D premiums.

The deduction of Medicare premiums affects beneficiaries differently, depending on their incomes and Social Security benefit amounts. Medicare premiums absorb a greater fraction of lower earners' Social Security benefits than of higher earners' benefits, because benefit amounts are progressive. However, some low-income beneficiaries are eligible for subsidies that cover their Medicare premiums and other out-of-pocket costs. Other beneficiaries with low benefits may be protected by a hold harmless provision that prevents a beneficiary's Social Security check from declining because of increases in the standard Part B premium.

Finally, it is important to note that although Social Security beneficiaries are affected by rising health-care costs, the benefits of participating in Medicare are substantially greater than the costs.

## INTRODUCTION

Social Security and Medicare are large and important parts of America's safety net. More than 40 million older and disabled individuals — about 1 in 7 Americans — are beneficiaries of both Social Security and Medicare.[1] Social

Security and Medicare account for a large amount of federal spending. In 2007, spending on the two programs was over $1 trillion, more than one-third of the federal budget and about 7% of gross domestic product (GDP), one measure of the size of the U.S. economy.[2]

Although Social Security and Medicare both play important roles in the well-being of older and disabled Americans, the interactions between the two programs are rarely examined. These interactions will become increasingly important as policymakers look for ways to slow the growth in spending on Social Security and Medicare. This chapter focuses on how Medicare premiums affect Social Security beneficiaries. Medicare premiums are rising faster than Social Security benefits, consequently consuming an increasing share of benefits over time.

Rising Medicare premiums could have a large effect on Social Security beneficiaries, particularly on those with low incomes and those who rely on Social Security as their primary source of income. Some beneficiaries will be able to pay for rising health-care costs; others may have limited resources. For example, among Americans aged 65 and older, about two-thirds receive more than half of their income from Social Security, and more than one-third receive more than 90% of their income from Social Security. These beneficiaries may see a decline in their standard of living as their Medicare premiums rise.

This chapter shows how the deduction of Medicare Part B and Part D premiums affects Social Security beneficiaries.[3] It describes how increases in Social Security benefits and Medicare premiums are calculated under current law and explains the circumstances under which Social Security beneficiaries are held harmless for increases in the standard Part B premium, as well as the premium assistance available to low-income beneficiaries. It shows the growth in Social Security benefits and Part B premiums in recent years and describes how rising Part B premiums have affected Social Security beneficiaries, comparing the effects of premium deductions on people with different levels of earnings. It also provides estimates of Social Security benefits and Medicare Parts B and D premiums to 2080, using the Social Security and Medicare trustees' intermediate projections, and describes how beneficiaries would be affected by projected Medicare premium increases. Finally, it outlines current legislation that would affect the relationship between Social Security benefits and Medicare premiums.

# BACKGROUND

## Social Security Benefits

Social Security provides retirement, disability, and survivors benefits to workers and their families. People become insured for benefits by working in Social Security- covered employment (i.e., by paying Social Security payroll taxes).[4] Generally, people who qualify for retirement benefits may receive reduced Social Security benefits as early as age 62 or full benefits at the full retirement age.[5] Those who qualify for disability or certain survivors benefits may receive them at any age. The amount of a worker's Social Security benefit is calculated by applying a progressive benefit formula to his or her lifetime earnings, adjusted for wage growth.[6] Historically, the average Social Security benefit paid to new beneficiaries has increased at about the same rate as average earnings.

### *Annual Cost-of-Living Adjustment (COLA)*

After a person becomes eligible to receive Social Security benefits, his or her monthly benefit amount is increased annually to maintain purchasing power over time. At the end of each year, the Social Security Administration (SSA) announces the cost-of-living adjustment (COLA) payable in January of the following year. The amount of the COLA is based on inflation as measured by the Consumer Price Index — Urban Wage Earners and Clerical Workers (CPI-W).[7]

### COLA for 2008

In January 2008, Social Security benefits increased by 2.3% for current beneficiaries. This benefit increase was based on the change in the CPI- W between October 2006 and September 2007. SSA estimated that the COLA increased the average retired worker's monthly benefit by $24.[8]

## Medicare Premiums

Medicare is the federal health insurance program for people aged 65 and older and for certain disabled people. Medicare is composed of four parts:

- Part A: Hospital Insurance (HI);

- Part B: Supplementary Medical Insurance (SMI), which covers physician services and other outpatient expenses;
- Part C: Medicare Advantage (MA), which covers the same services as Parts A and B through private health insurance plans; and
- Part D: covers prescription drugs through private plans.

Participation in Part A is required for Social Security beneficiaries aged 65 and older and for those who have received disability benefits for more than 24 months.[9] Part A beneficiaries may choose to participate in Parts B, C, and D.[10]

Medicare is funded through a combination of payroll taxes, general revenues, and beneficiary premiums. Medicare Part A is funded primarily through the payroll taxes of current workers and their employers, which are credited to the HI trust fund.[11] Parts B and D are financed through a combination of beneficiary premiums and federal general revenues, which are credited to the SMI trust fund. Part C is financed through the HI and SMI trust funds; Part C participants must pay the Part B premium.[12] Because this chapter focuses on the payment of Medicare premiums, the analysis herein primarily relates to Parts B and D.

### *Part B Premiums*

At the end of each year, the Centers for Medicare and Medicaid Services (CMS) announce Part B premiums for the next year. The Balanced Budget Act of 1997 permanently set the standard Part B premium to cover 25% of projected per capita Part B program costs for beneficiaries aged 65 and older.[13] If projected Part B costs increase or decrease, the premium rises or falls proportionately. Starting in 2007, higher-income beneficiaries pay higher Part B premiums.[14] An estimated 5% of Part B beneficiaries must pay income-related premiums in 2008.[15] Unless they qualify for low-income assistance, Part B participants must pay monthly premiums; they must also pay other out-of-pocket costs when they use Part B services.

### Part B Premiums for 2008

In January 2008, the standard Part B premium rose to $96.40 per month, an increase of 3.1% over 2007. The premium increase was necessary to cover the rising cost of Part B services and to build up trust fund reserves. In 2008, individuals whose modified adjusted gross income (AGI) exceeds $82,000, and couples whose modified AGI exceeds $164,000, are subject to higher premium amounts, as shown in **Table 1** below.[16] The analysis in this chapter focuses on the standard Part B premium, which is paid by most beneficiaries. In addition to premiums, Part B beneficiaries must also pay other out-of-pocket costs when they use services. The annual deductible for Part B services is $135 in 2008. After the annual deductible is met, beneficiaries are responsible for coinsurance costs, which are generally 20% of Medicare-approved Part B expenses.

### *Part D Premiums*

Medicare Part D was established in the Medicare Prescription Drug, Improvement, and Modernization Act of 2003 (MMA, P.L. 108- 173) and began covering beneficiaries' prescription drugs through private plans in January 2006.[17] To participate in Part D, qualified individuals must enroll in a participating prescription drug plan. Unless they qualify for low-income assistance, Part D participants must pay monthly premiums; they must also pay other out-of- pocket costs when they use Part D services.

MMA established guidelines for *standard* Part D coverage, including specific deductible and coinsurance amounts and a formula for calculating average premiums. Individual prescription drug plans are also allowed to offer *alternative* coverage that has at least actuarially equivalent benefits. In other words, alternative coverage plans must pay, on average, equal or greater benefits per person than standard coverage plans. Alternative coverage plans may charge higher or lower premiums, deductibles, and coinsurance than standard coverage plans.[18] This chapter focuses on beneficiaries' premiums for *standard* Part D coverage, which vary by plan. On average, a beneficiary's premium covers 25.5% of the value of a standard coverage plan and the federal government pays for the remaining 74.5%.

### Part D Premiums for 2008

The average premium for standard Part D coverage is $27.93 in 2008. The annual deductible for standard coverage is $275 in 2008. After meeting the deductible, beneficiaries pay 25% coinsurance costs for drug costs up to $2,510, all of their drug costs between $2,510 and $5,726, and about 5% of drug costs above $5,726.[19]

### *Medicare Advantage (Part C)*

Beneficiaries who are entitled to Medicare Part A and enrolled in Part B may choose to enroll in a private health insurance plan through Part C, also known as Medicare Advantage (MA), which provides healthcare coverage in lieu of traditional Medicare. In 2007, about 20% of Medicare beneficiaries were enrolled in Part C, mostly in managed care plans.[20] Medicare Advantage plans are generally required to offer the same services as Medicare Parts A and B. MA managed care organizations must also offer at least one Medicare Advantage-prescription drug plan (MA-PD) that includes drug coverage at least equivalent to standard coverage in Part D plans. (Beneficiaries enrolled in MA managed care plans may not enroll in a stand-alone Part D plan.)[21]

### Part C Premiums

Medicare Advantage participants' total premium amounts may be higher or lower than the Part B premium. Although the law requires that MA participants pay the Part B premium, some plans subsidize the premium for their enrollees. Other plans require that enrollees pay the full Part B premium plus an additional premium directly to the plan sponsor.[22]

#### *Premium Subsidies for Low-Income Beneficiaries*

The analysis in this chapter focuses on Social Security beneficiaries who pay Medicare premiums. However, low-income individuals (including MA participants) may qualify for low- income subsidies, which cover all or part of their Part B and Part D premiums.[23] About one in five of Medicare beneficiaries receive full Part B subsidies.

**Table 1. Part B Premiums, 2008**

| Modified Adjusted Gross Income (AGI) | | Premium |
|---|---|---|
| **Single** | **Couple** | |
| $82,000 or less | $164,000 or less | $96.40 |
| $82,001-$102,000 | $164,001-$204,000 | $122.20 |
| $102,001-$153,000 | $204,001-$306,000 | $160.90 |
| $153,001-$205,000 | $306,001-$410,000 | $199.70 |
| More than $205,000 | More than $410,000 | $238.40 |

Source: Social Security Administration, *Medicare Part B Premiums: Important Information For People Newly Eligible For Medicare 2008*, December 2007, at [http://www.ssa.gov/pubs/1 01 62.html].

Note: For more, see CRS Report RL32582, *Medicare: Part B Premiums*, by Jennifer O'Sullivan.

To qualify for subsidies, beneficiaries must have limited income and assets. Beneficiaries may qualify for full Part B premium subsidies if they have incomes of less than 135% of poverty and assets of less than $4,000 for an individual or $6,000 for a couple. Beneficiaries may qualify for full or partial Part D premium subsidies if they have incomes of less than 150% of poverty and assets of less than $11,990 for an individual and $23,970 for a couple in 2008.

Some beneficiaries who qualify for premium subsidies do not apply for them. For example, CMS has estimated that more than one-fourth of Medicare beneficiaries (roughly 11 million) qualify for full Part B subsidies.[24] In 2005, about two-thirds of qualifying individuals (7.5 million) received Part B subsidies.[25] CMS has also estimated that about a third of Medicare beneficiaries (roughly 14 million) qualify for full or partial Part D subsidies. In 2007, about 9.1 million beneficiaries received Part D subsidies, and an additional million low-income beneficiaries receive comprehensive drug coverage for little or no cost.[26] However, 3.3 million individuals eligible for subsidies had neither signed up for Part D nor had coverage through another source.

## Relationship between Social Security Benefits and Medicare Premiums

Ultimately, everyone who is eligible for Social Security retirement or disability benefits qualifies for Medicare.[27] Most people who participate in both programs pay Medicare premiums.[28] By law, the Medicare Part B premium is automatically deducted from the Social Security benefits of those enrolled in Part B (including MA and MA-PD participants).[29] Medicare Part D participants may choose to have their Part D premiums deducted from their benefits or to pay them directly to their prescription drug plan sponsors.

### Growth in Social Security Benefits and Part B Premiums

Historically, the growth in Medicare Part B premiums has greatly exceeded the growth in Social Security benefits. Over the past decade, Social Security's annual COLA resulted in a cumulative benefit increase of about 26%; average worker benefits have increased by about 34%.[30] At the same time, standard Part B premiums have more than doubled, from $45.50 in 1999 to $96.40 in 2008. By law, all Part B premiums are set as a proportion of projected Part B program costs. Part B costs — like all health-care costs — have been rising dramatically. This cost growth is driven by many factors, including increasing life expectancy, new medical technology, program expansion, increases in the earnings of health professionals, and other medical price growth (which has been higher than overall inflation).

The cumulative growth in standard Part B premiums has been dramatic, but annual changes have been somewhat erratic. During the past 10 years, annual Part B premium increases have ranged from 0% to more than 17%. Social Security COLAs, meanwhile, have ranged from 1.3% to 4.1%. **Figure 1** shows the annual rates of increase in Medicare premiums and Social Security benefits from 1999 to 2008.

## Hold Harmless Provision

A *hold harmless* provision reduces the Part B premium for beneficiaries whose Social Security COLAs are not sufficient to cover the standard Part B premium increase.[31] If, in a given year, the increase in the standard Part B premium would cause a beneficiary's Social Security check to be less than it was the year before, the premium is reduced to ensure that the nominal amount of the individual's Social Security check stays the same.[32] (See the **text box** below for an example.) However, high-income individuals who must pay income-related Part B premiums are *not* subject to the hold harmless provision. This means that for these high-income beneficiaries, Social Security checks can be reduced from one year to the next as a result of an increase in the Part B premium.

SSA determines which beneficiaries will be held harmless each year. In some cases, a beneficiary may be held harmless one year but not the next. In other cases, a beneficiary will be held harmless entirely because his or her premium was reduced in a previous year. The cumulative effect of the hold harmless provision can produce substantial savings for individuals with low benefits.

## Example of Hold Harmless Provision

To see the effect of the hold harmless provision, consider an individual, Maria, who retires in 2005 with a monthly Social Security benefit of $200. In 2005, Maria would receive a benefit check of $121. (Maria's 2005 check is equal to her benefit amount of $200, minus the 2005 Part B premium of $78.20, rounded down to the nearest dollar.)

In 2006, the inflation rate used to calculate the Social Security COLA was 4.1%. Thus, Maria's COLA for 2006 would have been $8.20 (4.1% times $200). The Part B premium for 2006 was $88.50 ($10.30 more than in 2005). If the *entire* Part B premium were deducted, Maria's check would fall from $121 in 2005 to $119 in 2006. (Maria's 2006 check is equal to her 2005 benefit amount of $200, plus the COLA of $8.20, minus the 2006 Part B premium of $88.50, rounded down to the nearest dollar.)

Because Maria's 2006 benefit check would be less than her 2005 benefit check (a result of the increase in the Part B premium), she would be held harmless. In other words, Maria's Part B premium would be reduced by $2, so that the nominal amount of her monthly Social Security check for 2006 would stay the same as it was in 2005 ($121).

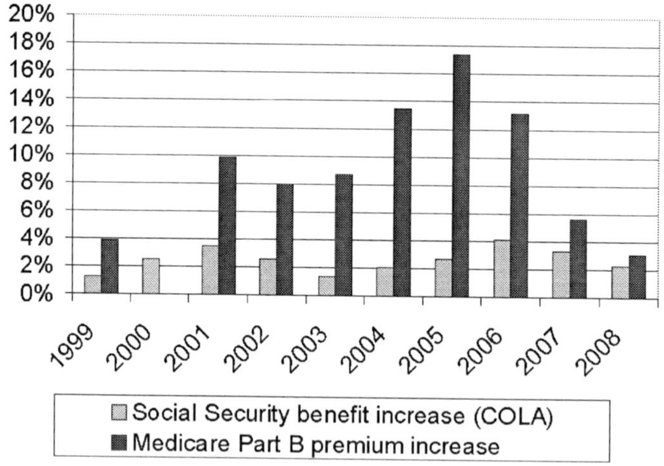


Source: Congressional Research Service calculations, based on figures from the *2007 Medicare Trustees Report* and the *2007 Social Security Trustees Report*.

Note: There was no increase in the Part B premium in 2000.

Figure 1. Annual Increase in Social Security Benefits and Standard Medicare Part B Premiums, 1999-2008

A beneficiary is *not* held harmless if the increase in his or her Part D premium (or the combined increase in Part B and Part D premiums) causes his or her Social Security check to decline. In other words, a person's Social Security check may decrease from one year to the next as a result of Part D premium increases.

Whether a beneficiary is held harmless depends on the amount of the standard Part B premium increase relative to the amount of his or her Social Security COLA in a given year. An individual's Social Security COLA is determined by multiplying his or her benefit amount by the inflation rate (i.e., the CPI-W). Part B premiums are determined by projected Part B program costs. Thus, the number of people held harmless can vary widely from year to year, depending on annual inflation rates and projected Part B costs. For example, about 1.8 million Part B participants (6% of those paying premiums) were held harmless in 2005, while roughly one million participants (3% of those paying premiums) were held harmless in 2006.[33] Low-income beneficiaries who are not required to pay Part B premiums are not affected by the hold harmless provision, nor are high-income beneficiaries who must pay income-related Part B premiums.

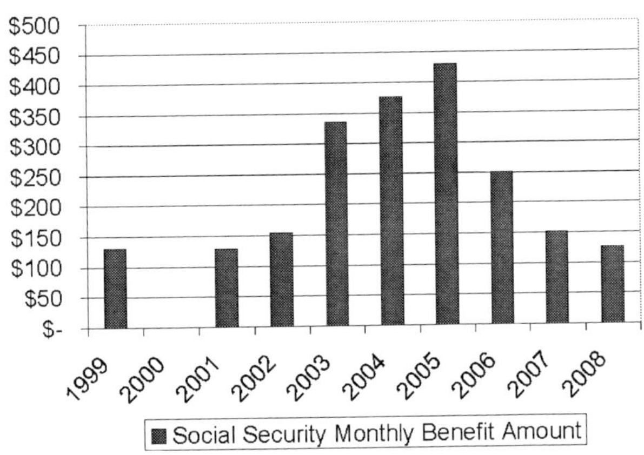


Source: Congressional Research Service calculations, based on figures from the *2007 Medicare Trustees Report* and the *2007 Social Security Trustees Report*.

Note: Some beneficiaries with benefits below the thresholds shown in this figure would not have had their Part B premiums reduced because their benefit checks would not have declined as a result of the Part B premium increase, due to the fact the Social Security benefits are rounded down to the nearest dollar. There was no increase in the Medicare Part B premium in 2000.

Figure 2. Approximate Thresholds for Hold Harmless Provision, 1999-2008

**Figure 2** shows the approximate thresholds beneath which Social Security beneficiaries who paid Part B premiums were held harmless from 1999 to 2008. The Part B premium increase is reduced for most beneficiaries with monthly Social Security benefits below the threshold in a given year.[34] If a beneficiary had benefits above the threshold in a given year, he or she would pay the full Part B premium increase in that year. In 2008, a beneficiary with a monthly Social Security benefit of less than $126 could be held harmless — that is, could pay a reduced Part B premium so that his or her Social Security checks would not decline due to the Part B premium increase.

# IMPACT OF MEDICARE PREMIUMS ON SOCIAL SECURITY BENEFICIARIES

## Actual Impact, 1999-2008

During the past decade, Medicare Part B premiums have absorbed a growing fraction of beneficiaries' Social Security benefits. The deduction of Part B premiums does not affect all beneficiaries equally. Paying the standard Part B premium, as most beneficiaries do, requires a relatively larger deduction from small Social Security benefits than from large benefits. Social Security benefits are based on workers' lifetime earnings; consequently, low earners are disproportionately affected by the deduction of Medicare premiums.

### *Effect of Part B Premiums on Social Security Benefits*

The following section illustrates how the deduction of Medicare Part B premiums would have affected the Social Security benefits of three hypothetical workers who retired in 1998: a low earner, a medium earner, and a high earner.[35] The *low earner* is assumed to have earned 45% of the average wage during each year of his or her career (about $19,000 in 2008) and to receive a monthly Social Security benefit of about $700 in 2008.[36] The *medium earner* is assumed to have earned the average wage during each year of his or her career (about $42,000 in 2008) and to receive a monthly Social Security benefit of about $1,200 in 2008. The *high earner* is assumed to have earned 160% of the average wage during each year of his or her career (about $68,000 in 2008) and to receive a monthly Social Security benefit of $1,500 in 2008. All of the hypothetical workers are assumed to have been born in 1930, to have worked full-time each year from age 22 to 65 with no interruptions, to have retired in 1998 at age 65, and to pay the standard Part B premium without low- income assistance.[37] **Figure 3** shows the percentage of each hypothetical worker's Social Security benefits deducted to pay the standard Part B premium from 1999 to 2008.

As shown in **Figure 3**, a growing proportion of Social Security benefits have been deducted to pay Part B premiums over the 10-year period. The proportion of Social Security benefits needed to pay the Part B premium was stable from 1999 to 2001, in part because there was no premium increase in 2000. During this period, the medium earner needed approximately 5% of his or her Social Security benefits to pay the Part B premium each year. As the Part B premium increased from 2001 to 2008, the proportion of Social Security benefits needed to pay the Part B premium rose substantially. By 2008, the Part B premium absorbed about 8% of the medium earner's benefits.

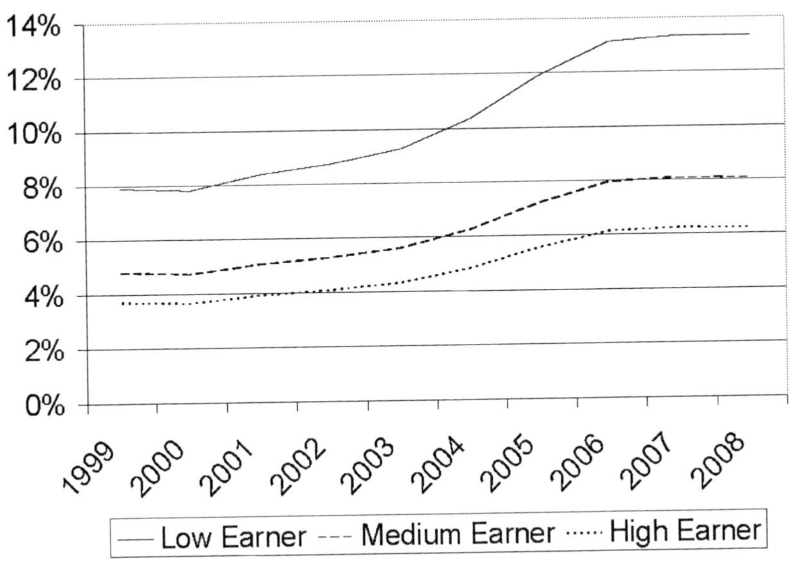


Source: Congressional Research Service calculations, based on figures from the *2007 Medicare Trustees Report* and the *2007 Social Security Trustees Report*.

Note: The calculations in this figure are based on individuals who retired in 1998. Estimates for other cohorts would vary.

Figure 3. Percentage of Total Social Security Benefits Deducted for Standard Part B Premiums, 1999-2008

Lower earners need a greater fraction of their Social Security benefits to pay the Part B premium than do higher earners. For example, in 2008 the low earner in this illustration needs about 13% of his or her Social Security benefits to pay the Part B premium. In contrast, the high earner needs about 6% of his or her benefits to pay the Part B premium.

### *Effect of Part B Premium Increases on Social Security COLAs*

The Social Security COLA is designed to ensure that Social Security benefits keep up with overall inflation. However, in some years, a disproportionate share of the COLA is absorbed by the increase in the Part B premium. In these years, beneficiaries' ability to pay for all other goods and services decreases.

Using the same three hypothetical workers as examples, **Figure 4** shows the percentage of the Social Security COLA absorbed by the annual increase in Medicare premiums in each year from 1999 to 2008. The proportion of the COLA needed to pay the increase in the Part B premium has varied substantially over time. In recent years, a large proportion of beneficiaries' COLAs have been absorbed by the Part B premium increase. For example, in 2004 and 2005 the Part B premium increase absorbed more than half of the medium earner's COLA. In 2008, the Part B premium increase absorbed about 8% of the medium earner's COLA.

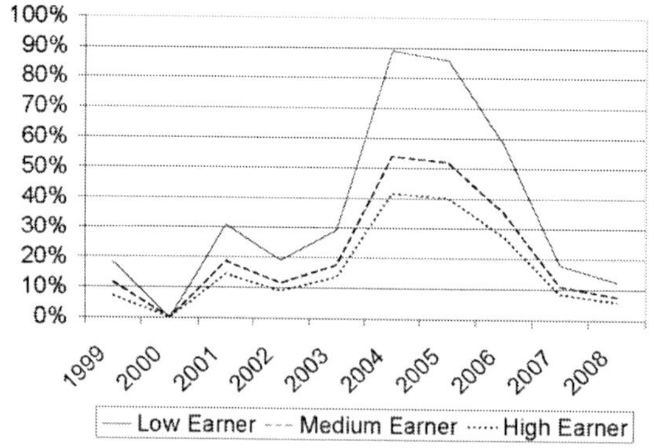


**Source:** Congressional Research Service calculations, based on figures from the *2007 Medicare Trustees Report* and the *2007 Social Security Trustees Report*.

**Note:** The calculations in this figure are based on individuals who retired in 1998. Estimates for other cohorts would vary.

Figure 4. Percentage of Social Security COLAs Absorbed by Standard Part B Increase, 1999-2008

Those with lower benefits need a greater fraction of their Social Security COLAs to cover the Part B premium increase than those with higher benefits. In 2008, the Part B premium increase absorbed about 13% of the low earner's COLA and about 6% of the high earner's COLA. None of the workers in this example would have been held harmless, because paying the full Part B premium increase would not have caused their benefit checks to decrease from any one year to the next.

## Future Impact, 2009-2080

Most experts agree that Medicare costs will continue to outstrip the growth in prices (and thus Social Security COLAs) and wages (and thus initial Social Security benefits). The trustees of Social Security and Medicare project that over the long term, annual inflation will average 2.8%, annual wage growth will average 3.9%, and annual increases in Parts B and D costs per beneficiary will average 5% or more. Long-range projections are inherently imprecise; the further into the future one looks, the wider the range of possible outcomes. Projections of Medicare cost growth are particularly uncertain. Sources of uncertainty range from the difficulty of predicting medical breakthroughs to the ongoing implementation of Part D.

### *Projected Effect of Part B Premiums on Social Security Benefits*

If Part B costs rise at the rate the trustees have projected, premiums will absorb an increasing share of beneficiaries' Social Security benefits. In fact, many experts believe that Part B costs will grow faster than the trustees have projected.

## Why the Trustees' Projections of Medicare Part B Premiums May Be Too Low

**Trustees Assume Cuts to Physician Payments**. The Medicare trustees make their projections of future program costs and premiums based on the provisions of the law that authorizes Medicare. The law requires a sustainable growth rate (SGR) formula to be used to calculate Medicare physician payments, which account for about 50% of Part B costs. Application of this formula would result in cuts to physician fees of about 5% each year until 2012. The Medicare trustees assume that these cuts will be made.

However, congressional action has prevented cuts to physician fees for 2003 to 2007. Many Members of Congress were concerned about the impact of potential payment reductions on beneficiaries' access to services. The trustees acknowledge that "multiple years of significant reductions in physician payments per service are very unlikely to occur before legislative changes intervene." If the trustees had *not* assumed that physician payments would be cut, projected Part B costs would be significantly higher. Consequently, projected Part B premiums would be higher, because they are proportionate to projected program costs.

**Trustees Assume Medicare Cost Growth Will Slow**. The Medicare trustees assume that the growth in Medicare costs (and thus premiums) will slow in the future. The Congressional Budget Office (CBO) explains that "in their long range forecasts, the Medicare trustees assume that the development and increasing use of new medical technologies will cause spending per enrollee to continue to grow faster than [inflation and wages] but that significant pressures will be brought to bear on the entire health-care system to reduce [costs]." Consequently, the trustees project that the growth in Medicare premiums will also slow. The trustees' intermediate projection is that Part B premiums will increase by an average annual rate of about 5% over the long term.

Many experts believe this projected growth rate is too low. One reason is that the trustees' projections are significantly lower than past growth rates for Part B premiums. If Part B premiums continue to rise at the same rate as they have in the past, they will increase much more rapidly than the Medicare trustees project.

Sources: CRS Report RL32582, *Medicare: Part B Premiums*, by Jennifer O'Sullivan; *2007 Medicare Trustees Report*; and CBO, *The Long-Term Budget Outlook*, December 2007.**Figure 5** shows the proportion of Social Security benefits that a hypothetical low, medium, and high earner would need to pay standard Part B premiums in each year from 2009 to 2080, using the trustees' intermediate projections. None of the workers were assumed to be subject to higher Part B premiums for high-income beneficiaries that began in 2007. Each year in the graph shows the projected percentage of Social Security benefits that each worker would need to pay Medicare premiums *if he or she turned 65 and retired in January of that year*.

The estimates in **Figures 5 and 6** show the proportion of *initial* Social Security benefits needed to pay Medicare premiums for a series of different cohorts. Initial Social Security benefits are indexed to wages. In contrast, the estimates in **Figure 3** show the proportion of Social Security benefits needed to pay Medicare premiums for a single cohort over time. After the initial year, benefits are indexed to inflation using the COLA. This difference is important because **Figure 3** compares Medicare premium growth to *price* growth (i.e., inflation), whereas **Figures 5 and 6** compare Medicare premium growth to *wage* growth. On average, Medicare premiums have grown faster than both wages and prices and are projected to do so in the future.

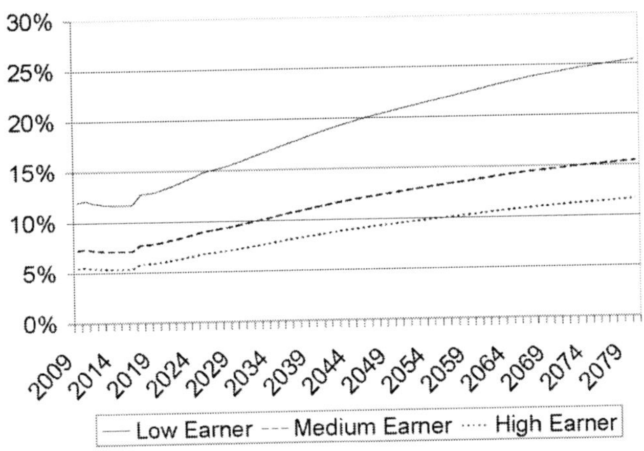


Source: Congressional Research Service calculations using intermediate projections from the *2007 Medicare Trustees Report* (data underlying figure III.C1, provided by CMS).

Note: Part B premiums are *not* expected to decrease as a proportion of Social Security benefits, as they are shown to do in the early years of **Figure 5**. **Figure 5** is based on the trustees' projections; the trustees acknowledge that their short-run projections of Part B costs are "unrealistically low" due to the assumption that physician payments will be cut (*2007 Medicare Trustees Report*, p. 21). In addition, **Figures 5 and 6** show a cohort of hypothetical workers *each year* in the first year of their retirements, whereas **Figure 3** shows a single cohort of hypothetical workers over time.

Figure 5. Percentage of Initial Social Security Benefits Deducted for Standard Medicare Part B Premiums, 2009-2080

Beneficiaries are projected to need a much larger fraction of their Social Security benefits to pay Part B premiums in the future. For example, the medium earner who retires in 2009 is projected to need 7% of his or her benefits to pay the Part B premium in the first year of retirement. The medium earner who retires in 2080 is projected to need more than twice that share, using 15% of his or her benefits to pay the Part B premium in the first year of retirement.

In the future, as in the past, low earners will need a greater fraction of their benefits to pay the Part B premium than will high earners. A low earner retiring in 2080 is projected to need 25% of his or her benefits to pay the Part B premium in the first year of retirement. In contrast, a high earner retiring in 2080 is projected to need 12% of his or her benefits to pay the Part B premium in the first year of retirement.

### *Projected Effect of Part D Premiums on Social Security Benefits*

Since Medicare Part D was implemented in 2006, it is difficult to project how it might change over time. (See the **text box** below.) Early estimates of Part D costs varied widely. The nature of Part D makes it difficult to project premiums, because individual plans set premiums for their beneficiaries. In general, prescription drug spending has been rising at least as much as overall health spending; this trend is expected to continue.[38]

## Uncertainties in Projecting Part D Premiums

**How will drug prices and utilization change?** Changes in drug prices and utilization could have a significant impact on Part D premiums. If generic drugs become increasingly available or more widely used, premiums could be lower than expected. Alternatively, pharmaceutical breakthroughs or increased use of expensive prescriptions could lead to higher premiums.

**How many prescription drug plans will compete for beneficiaries?** In the first several years of implementation, a greater-than-expected number of plans offered Part D benefits. If a large number of plans continue to offer Part D benefits, competition to attract beneficiaries could drive down premiums. Alternatively, some analysts believe that the fierce competition for beneficiaries will force some plans out of Part D in future years, reducing competition and leading to higher premiums.

**Figure 6** shows the proportion of Social Security benefits needed to pay *combined* Part B and Part D premiums for hypothetical workers retiring in each year from 2009 to 2080, using the trustees' intermediate projections. Each year in the graph shows the projected percentage of Social Security benefits that a low, medium, and high earner would need to pay Medicare premiums if he or she turned 65 and retired in January of that year. All beneficiaries are assumed to pay the standard Part B premium as well as the *average* premium for *standard* Part D coverage. In interpreting **Figure 6**, it is important to note that Part D premiums vary widely by plan, and that Part D premiums may be deducted from beneficiaries' Social Security checks or be paid directly to the plan.

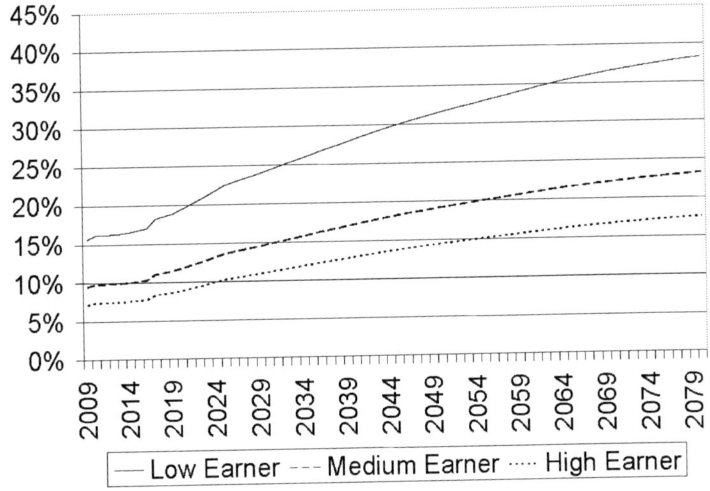


Source: Congressional Research Service calculations using intermediate projections from the *2007 Medicare Trustees Report* (data underlying figure III.C1, provided by CMS).

Note: Part B premiums are *not* expected to decrease as a proportion of Social Security benefits, as they are shown to do in the early years of **Figure 5**. **Figure 5** is based on the trustees' projections; the trustees acknowledge that their short-run projections of Part B costs are "unrealistically low" due to the assumption that physician payments will be cut (*2007 Medicare Trustees Report*, p. 21). In addition, **Figures 5 and 6** show a cohort of hypothetical workers *each year* in the first year of their retirements, whereas **Figure 3** shows a single cohort of hypothetical workers over time.

Figure 6. Percentage of Initial Social Security Benefits Deducted for Standard Part B and D Premiums, 2009-2080

Together, Part B and Part D premiums are projected to consume an increasing share of beneficiaries' Social Security benefits over time. For example, the medium earner retiring in 2009 is projected to need 9% of benefits to pay Parts B and D premiums in the first year of retirement. The medium earner retiring in 2080 is projected to need more than twice that share, using 23% of benefits to pay Parts B and D premiums in the first year of retirement.

Low earners will need a greater proportion of their Social Security benefits to pay for combined Parts B and D premiums than will high earners. A low earner who retires in 2080 is projected to need about 38% his or her Social Security benefits to pay Parts B and D premiums in the first year of retirement. In contrast, a high earner who retires in 2080 is projected to need 18% of his or her benefits to pay Parts B and D premiums in the first year of retirement.

## LEGISLATION IN THE 110TH CONGRESS

Any changes to the way Medicare premiums or Social Security benefits are calculated would also change the number of beneficiaries held harmless. To date, there are two bills in the 110th Congress that would hold more Social Security beneficiaries harmless for increases in Medicare premiums.

**H.R. 4807**, introduced by Representative Stephanie Herseth Sandlin, and **S. 2501**, introduced by Senator Tim Johnson, would extend the current law hold harmless provision to apply to increases in Medicare Part D premiums. In addition, these bills would limit the combined annual increase in the Part B premium and the average Part D premium for standard coverage to 25% of each beneficiary's annual Social Security COLA. By including Part D premiums in the hold harmless provision and limiting the proportion of the COLA used to pay for premium increases, H.R. 3954 and S. 1795 would raise the thresholds at which beneficiaries are held harmless. As a result, more beneficiaries would be held harmless, and part of these beneficiaries' premium costs could be shifted to Medicare. No cost estimates for these bills are available at the time of this writing.

## CONCLUSION

Rising Medicare premiums are consuming a growing share of beneficiaries' Social Security benefits. An increasing number of Americans will be affected by this interaction as the number of Social Security and Medicare beneficiaries grows over time. The Social Security trustees project that by 2050, the proportion of Americans aged 65 and older — most of whom are eligible for both Social Security and Medicare — will almost double.[39]

Low-income beneficiaries and those who rely primarily on Social Security may see a decline in their standard of living as their Medicare expenses rise. Premiums for Parts B and D are projected to increase significantly faster than Social Security benefits. Out-of-pocket costs for Parts B and D are projected to grow at the same rates as premiums, contributing to the growing health-care expenses of beneficiaries. Most beneficiaries are likely to have income apart from their Social Security benefits. However, many of tomorrow's beneficiaries, like today's, are likely to rely mostly on Social Security, especially as traditional pension coverage declines and many Americans save little or nothing for retirement.[40] These beneficiaries could struggle to cover their health-care expenses.

Rising health-care costs have serious consequences, not just for Social Security beneficiaries, but for everyone who pays health-care costs. Premiums for employer- sponsored health insurance are also rising faster than wages and inflation, which contributes to the declining number of employers offering health insurance coverage, from 69% in 2000 to 60% in 2007.[41] About one-fifth of Americans under age 65 have no health insurance coverage.[42]

Federal and state budgets are also struggling to meet growing health-care costs. CBO projects that Medicare's costs will more than triple as a share of the economy by 2050.[43] Similarly, CBO projects that the federal costs of Medicaid, the federal- state low-income health-care program, will more than double as a share of the economy; growth will cause similar strains for state budgets. Growth of this magnitude has important economic effects. According to CBO, the rate at which health-care costs grow relative to national income is the most important factor affecting the nation's long-term fiscal outlook.[44]

Finally, it is important to remember that Social Security beneficiaries gain from their participation in the Medicare program. Medicare provides health-care coverage to the vast majority of Americans aged 65 and older and to most disability beneficiaries. Together, Medicare and Medicaid cover a majority of participating Social Security beneficiaries' health-care expenses. Although

Social Security beneficiaries are affected by rising health-care costs, the benefits of participating in Medicare are substantially greater than the costs.

## End Notes

[1] Social Security Administration, *2007 Annual Report of the Board of Trustees of the Federal Old-Age and Survivors Insurance and Disability Insurance Trust Funds*, May 1, 2007, at [http://www.ssa.gov/OACT/TR/TR07/tr07.pdf]. (Hereafter cited as *2007 Social Security Trustees Report.*) Centers for Medicare and Medicaid Services, *2007 Annual Report of the Boards of Trustees of the Federal Hospital Insurance and Federal Supplementary Medical Insurance Trust Funds*, May 1, 2007, available at [http://www.cms.hhs.gov/ReportsTrustFunds/downloads/tr2007.pdf]. (Hereafter cited as *2007 Medicare Trustees Report.*)

[2] Congressional Budget Office, *The Budget and Economic Outlook: An Update*, August 23, 2007, at [http://www.cbo.gov/ftpdocs/77xx/doc773 1/01 -24-BudgetOutlook.pdf].

[3] Medicare Part B, Supplementary Medical Insurance (SMI), covers physician services and other outpatient expenses. Medicare Part D covers prescription drugs through private plans.

[4] The amount of time a person must work in Social Security-covered employment to be insured for benefits depends on the type of benefit, among other factors. For more details, see CRS Report 94-27, *Social Security: Brief Facts and Statistics*, by Gary Sidor.

[5] The age at which workers may receive full retirement benefits is rising from 65 (for those born before 1938) to 67 (for those born after 1959).

[6] Social Security benefits provided to a worker's family, such as spouse benefits and survivor benefits, are based on the lifetime earnings of the worker. For more information, see CRS Report 94-27, *Social Security: Brief Facts and Statistics*, by Gary Sidor.

[7] The CPI-W tracks the prices of a fixed market basket of goods and services over time. Social Security's COLA is calculated as the change in the CPI-W from the third quarter of the prior calendar year to the third quarter of the current calendar year. If the CPI-W increases during this period, Social Security benefits for the next year increase proportionately. If the CPI-W decreases, Social Security benefits stay the same. See CRS Report 94-803, *Social Security: The Cost-of-Living Adjustment in January 2008*, by Gary Sidor and CRS Report RL3 0074, *The Consumer Price Index: A Brief Overview*, by Brian W. Cashell.

[8] Social Security Administration, *2008 Social Security Changes*, October 2007, at [http://www.ssa.gov/pressoffice/factsheets/colafacts2008.htm].

[9] People who receive Social Security benefits that confer eligibility for Part A (i.e., retirement benefits for those aged 65 and older and disability benefits after 24 months) may not waive Part A entitlement. (Social Security Administration, Program Operations Manual System, HI 00801.002, at [https://s044a90.ssa.gov/apps 1 0/poms.nsf/lnx/060080 1002! opendocument].)

[10] Of Part A beneficiaries, roughly 94% are enrolled in Part B, and about 20% are enrolled in Part C. In 2007, about 90% of Medicare beneficiaries had prescription drug coverage of some kind. About 55% were enrolled in stand-alone Part D plans or had prescription drug coverage through their Part C plans, and an additional 34% were enrolled in other health insurance plans that were subsidized by Part D. (CRS Report RL34280, *Medicare Part D Prescription Drug Benefit: A Primer*, by Jennifer O'Sullivan.)

[11] About 99% of Medicare beneficiaries qualify for premium-free Part A coverage, which they earn if they (or their spouses) have worked at least 10 years in Medicare-covered employment. Individuals without sufficient work history who are otherwise eligible for Medicare may participate in the program if they pay monthly Part A premiums.

[12] The law requires that Part C participants pay the Part B premium. Some Part C plans subsidize the premium for their enrollees; others require that enrollees pay the full Part B premium plus an additional premium directly to the plan sponsor.

[13] Disabled Medicare beneficiaries under age 65 pay the same premium amount as those aged 65 or older, though their per capita Part B costs are higher.

[14] The Medicare Prescription Drug, Improvement, and Modernization Act of 2003 (P.L. 108-173) increased the Part B premium percentage for high-income enrollees; the Deficit Reduction Act of 2005 (P.L.109-171) accelerated the phase-in period for such premiums.

[15] SSA, *Medicare Part B Premiums: Important Information For People Newly Eligible For Medicare 2008*, December 2007, at [http://www.ssa.gov/pubs/10162.html].

[16] For more information, see CRS Report RL32582, *Medicare: Part B Premiums*, by Jennifer O'Sullivan.

[17] See CRS Report RL3 1966, *Overview of the Medicare Prescription Drug, Improvement, and Modernization Act of 2003*, by Jennifer O'Sullivan, et al., and CRS Report RL3 1525, *Beneficiary Cost-Sharing Under the Medicare Prescription Drug Benefit*, by Jim Hahn.

[18] For example, in 2008 premiums for stand-alone Part D plans ranged from $9.80 to $107.50 per month. (Kaiser Family Foundation, *Medicare Part D 2008 Data Spotlight: Premiums*, November 2007, at [http://www.kff.org/medicare/upload/7706.pdf].)

[19] The majority of plans offered to beneficiaries in 2006 were alternative coverage plans. Many of these plans include tiered cost-sharing, under which costs are lower for generic drugs and higher for brand-name drugs.

[20] Kaiser Family Foundation, *Fact Sheet: Medicare Advantage*, June 2007, at [http://www.kff.org/medicare/upload/2052-10.pdf].

[21] MA providers of nonmanaged care plans (i.e., private fee-for-service [PFFS] plans and medical savings accounts [MSAs]) are *not* required to offer prescription drug coverage. Drug coverage is optional for PFFS providers; PFFS plan enrollees without drug coverage are permitted to enroll in a stand-alone Part D plan. MSAs may not offer drug coverage.

[22] As of 2006, the majority (55%) of MA participants' total premiums were equal to the Part B premium amount, then $88.50 per month. About 42% of MA participants paid higher premiums, and about 3% paid lower premiums. On average, MA participants' total monthly premiums were about $26 more than the Part B premium. (AARP Public Policy Institute, *2006 Medicare Advantage Benefits and Premiums,* by Marsha Gold, Maria Cupples Hudson, and Sarah Davis, November 2006, at [http://assets.aarp.org/rgcenter/health/2006_23_ medicare.pdf].)

[23] For more information on subsidies for low-income Medicare beneficiaries, see CRS Report RL32582, *Medicare: Part B Premiums* and CRS Report RL3 2902, *Medicare Prescription Drug Benefit: Low-Income Provisions*, both by Jennifer O'Sullivan.

[24] Centers for Medicare and Medicaid Services, *Over 38 Million People with Medicare Now Receiving Prescription Drug Coverage*, June 14, 2006, at [http://hhs.gov/news/press/2006 pres/200606 14.html].

[25] Kaiser Commission on Medicaid and the Uninsured, *Dual Eligibles: Medicaid's Role for Low-Income Medicare Beneficiaries*, February 2006, at [http://www.kff.org/medicaid/ upload/Dual-Eligibles-Medicaid-s-Role-for-Low-Income-Medicare-Beneficiaries-Feb-20 06.pdf]. (Hereafter cited as Kaiser, *Dual Eligibles.*)

[26] Centers for Medicare and Medicaid Services, *Medicare Drug Plans Strong and Growing*, January 30, 2007, available at [http://www.cms.hhs.gov/apps/media/press/release.asp? Counter=2079&intNumPerPage=1 0&checkDate=&checkKey=&srchType=1 &numDays =3500&srchOpt=0&srchData=&keywordType=All&chkNewsType=1%2C+2%2C+3%2 C+4%2C+5&intPage=&showAll=&pYear=&year=&desc=false&cboOrder=date].

[27] People aged 65 and older who qualify for Social Security benefits and people of any age who receive disability benefits (after a two-year waiting period) are entitled to Part A and are also eligible to enroll in Part B, in a private health insurance plan through Part C, and/or in a private prescription drug plan through Part D.

[28] Some beneficiaries do not pay Medicare premiums, either because they receive low- income assistance or because they choose not to enroll in Medicare Part B or Part D.

[29] 42 U.S.C. § 1 840(a)( 1). Part B premiums are also deducted from Railroad Retirement benefits (42 U.S.C. § 1840(b)(1)).

[30] The COLA increases the benefits paid to *current* beneficiaries. In contrast, average Social Security benefits (those paid to new and current beneficiaries) have risen at a faster rate than the annual COLA, because the formula for calculating initial Social Security benefits is linked to *wage* growth, whereas the COLA is based on *price* growth. Generally, wages rise faster than prices.

[31] 42 U.S.C. § 1839(f). The hold harmless provision was first implemented in January 1987.

[32] To be held harmless in a given year, a beneficiary must have had Part B premiums deducted from both the December check of the prior year and the January check of the current year. Changes in a beneficiary's benefit amount (other than the COLA) do not affect whether the beneficiary is held harmless. If a beneficiary's benefit amount changes during a year in which he or she is held harmless (e.g., a beneficiary starts to receive a government pension offset), the Part B premium amount does *not* change. For more information on the hold harmless provision, see Social Security Administration, *Variable Supplementary Medical Insurance Premiums*, Actuarial Note No. 147, by Jacqueline A. Walsh and Burt M. Kestenbaum, March 2006, at [http://www.ssa.gov/OACT/NOTES/pdf_notes/note147.pdf]. (Hereafter cited as SSA Actuarial Note No. 147.)

[33] SSA Actuarial Note No. 147.

[34] Some beneficiaries with benefits below these thresholds would *not* have had their Part B premiums reduced because their benefit checks would not have declined as a result of the Part B premium increase, due to the fact the Social Security benefits are rounded down to the nearest dollar. These thresholds apply only to beneficiaries who were not held harmless in the previous year. For more information, see SSA Actuarial Note No. 147.

[35] The hypothetical workers were developed by SSA's actuaries. See Social Security Administration, Office of the Chief Actuary, Actuarial Note Number 144, *Internal Rates of Return Under the OASDI Program for Hypothetical Workers*, by Orlo R. Nichols, et al., June 2001, at [http://www.ssa.gov/OACT/NOTES/note2000s/note144.html].

[36] The *average wage* is defined by SSA's Average Wage Index (AWI). The AWI tends to overestimate workers' lifetime earnings. See University of Michigan Retirement Research Center, Working Paper WP 2004-074, *Modeling Lifetime Earnings Paths: Hypothetical versus Actual Workers*, by Andrew Au, Olivia Mitchell, and John W.R. Phillips, March 2004, at [http://www.mrrc.isr.umich.edu/publications/Papers/pdf/wp074.pdf].

[37] The low earner could potentially qualify for assistance in paying Part B premiums if he or she had little or no income besides Social Security benefits, had assets below the statutory limit ($4,000 for an individual and $6,000 for a couple), and applied for assistance.

[38] Borger, Christine, et al., "Health Spending Projections Through 2015: Changes on the Horizon," *Health Affairs* (25), February 22, 2006, available at [http://content.health affairs.org/cgi/reprint/25/2/w61].

[39] *2007 Social Security Trustees Report.*

[40] CRS Report RL30122, *Pension Sponsorship and Participation: Summary of Recent Trends*; CRS Report RL30922, *Retirement Savings and Household Wealth: A Summary of Recent Data*, both by Patrick Purcell.

[41] Kaiser Family Foundation and Health Research and Educational Trust, *Employer Health Benefits: 2007 Annual Survey*, September 2007, at [http://www.kff.org/insurance/7672/ upload/76723 .pdf].

[42] CRS Report 96-891, *Health Insurance Coverage: Characteristics of the Insured and Uninsured Populations in 2006,* by Chris L. Peterson and April Grady.

[43] For 2007, Medicare costs were 2.7% of GDP; the entire federal budget was 20% of GDP. For 2050, projected Medicare costs are 8.9% of GDP. (Congressional Budget Office, *The Long-*

*Term Budget Outlook*, December 2007, at [http://www.cbo.gov/ftpdocs/88xx/doc 8877/12-13-LTBO.pdf]. Hereafter cited as *CBO Long-Term Outlook*, 2007.)

[44] *CBO Long-Term Outlook*, 2007.

In: The Role of Savings and Other Issues... ISBN: 978-1-60741-446-9
Editor: Joel K. Harris 

*Chapter 2*

# IRAs and Other Savings Incentives: A Brief Overview*

*Jane G. Gravelle*

## Summary

Several types of savings are eligible for beneficial treatment under the individual income tax, and Individual Retirement Accounts (IRAs) have received considerable attention. Pension savings are actually more important in terms of revenue loss. There are other investments that are treated favorably as well. The President has proposed in a succession of budgets to significantly expand IRAs. Effects of these provisions on savings are uncertain, and, despite dollar limits on contributions and income phase outs, IRAs tend to benefit higher income individuals.

## Description of Tax Treatment

Several types of investments are preferentially treated under the individual income tax, including Individual Retirement Accounts (IRAs), pensions,

* This is an edited, reformatted and augmented version of a CRS Report for Congress publication dated March 2008.

capital gains, dividends, owner occupied housing, and life insurance policy earnings.

There are two types of IRAs that have the effect of exempting investment earnings from tax — the traditional (deductible) IRA and the Roth IRA. For the deductible IRA (also called a front-loaded IRA), contributions are deducted when made and withdrawals are taxed; this treatment is similar to the treatment of pensions. Eligibility for the deductible IRA is phased out as income increases for individuals who are active participants in employer pension plans. (Individuals above the income phase-out can make non-deductible contributions, with earnings taxed when withdrawn, which allows deferral, but not elimination, of taxes.) There are penalties for early withdrawal and mandatory distribution requirements.

As described above, IRAs were treated the same way as pension plans, with contributions deductible and withdrawals taxable. The Roth IRA (also called a back- loaded IRA), was added as an option in 1997, when eligibility for both types of IRAs was expanded. The tax treatment of this account is similar to that of a tax exempt bond: earnings are simply not taxed. The earnings phase-outs are higher and treatment is, in general, more generous than in the case of the deductible IRA. The annual deduction limit for IRA contributions when expanded in 1997 was the lesser of $2,000 or 100% of compensation; that limit was increased under the temporary provisions of the 2001 tax cut and eventually made permanent at $5,000.

The 2001 act also introduced a tax credit for contributions by low income individuals.

Favorable tax treatment of pensions, namely allowing the firm to deduct contributions which are not included in employees income and exempting the earnings of pension trusts as in the case of deductible IRAs, has been in place almost since the inception of the tax law. Pensions fall into two types: defined benefit plans where payments depend on earnings and years of service at retirement, and defined contribution plans where payments depend on the amount accumulated in an account. Pensions are subject to many rules and regulations designed to ensure that tax benefits do not accrue to owners and highly compensated managers and that pension trusts are adequately funded in the case of defined benefit plans. Of course to the extent that pension assets (or IRA assets) are invested in corporate stock, tax is collected at the corporate level.

Tax benefits for pension plans are much more important in dollar terms than are tax benefits for IRAs. For FY2009, according the latest Joint Committee on Taxation (JCT) estimates, employer pensions resulted in a revenue loss of $120.4 billion, with plans for self-employed individuals (called Keogh plans) costing $9.5 billion. IRAs resulted in a loss of $18.5 billion.[1] In the case of dividends, about half of the income is not subject to tax because of tax preferred status.

There are other savings and investments that receive favorable treatment under the individual income tax. Capital gains has historically been favorably treated, both through lower tax rates, deferral (taxed only when realized), and forgiveness of tax if passed on at death. Dividends are also now eligible for lower tax rates. Of course, earnings on corporate stock are taxed under the corporate tax. Owner occupied housing is also favorably treated because imputed rent is not included in income, and earnings on investments in life insurance policies are deferred and, when passed on via death benefits, exempt from tax. These tax benefits are significant as well. Lower rates for capital gains and dividends are estimated by the JCT to lose $131.0 billion in FY2009, the failure to tax gains at death $57.5 billion, and the deferral of gain for gifts $5.9 billion. While there is not a separate estimate for excluding imputed rent, the value of deducting costs (even though gross rent is not included in income) through itemized deductions is $85.2 billion for mortgage interest and $14.2 billion for property taxes. The exemption of most capital gains on homes is estimated to cost $30.1 billion. The value of deferral and forgiveness of earnings on life insurance policies is $27.5 billion.

## RECENT LEGISLATIVE ACTIVITY

IRAs were expanded by the 2001 tax bill, H.R. 1836, which was signed into law on June 7, 2001. IRA limits increased to $3,000 in 2002, $4,000 in 2005 and $5,000 in 2008, with indexation afterwards. Individual 50 and over had an extra $500 increase in 2002 and will have a $1,000 increase in 2008. This bill also increased contribution limits for pension plans, including 401(k) plans. Because of budget rules the tax cuts in this bill were sunsetted in 2010, but the increased limit was made permanent by the Pension Protection Act of 2006. The Pension Protection Act also allowed a rollover of IRA amounts to charity for those aged 70 and 1/2 without incurring tax effects.[2] This provision expired after 2007 but may be reinstated along with other extenders.

President Bush proposed in his FY2004 through FY2009 budget plans to eliminate the deductible IRA form. His proposal would rename the Roth IRAs as Retirement Savings Accounts (RSAs), and also allow Lifetime Savings

Accounts (LSAs).[3] The contribution limits would be greatly increased (to $5,000 for each type of account under the most recent proposal) and the income limits would be eliminated. Individuals could roll over existing accounts into these new accounts, by paying tax on the rollovers, which would increase revenue in the short run. The latest proposal is expected to initially gain and then lose revenue, with loss in the tenth year of $.5 billion. In the long run, the provision would cost much more. His proposal would also combine a variety of employer savings accounts into a single account and simplify the rules designed to prevent discrimination in favor of highly compensated employees. This proposal might form part of an the President's proposal for fundamental tax reform.

The Enron scandal and the slow recovery of the economy led to legislative proposals regarding pensions in the 107th Congress that did not see completion and were not addressed in the 108th Congress. However, the Pension Protection Act of 2006 eventually provided a variety of revisions and liberalizations of pension policy.

## ISSUES

The original rationale for IRAs, first introduced in 1962, was to provide parity with individuals covered by employer pensions. IRAs were made universally available in 1981, with the primary rationale to encourage savings. Income limits that disallowed deductible IRA coverage for most individuals were adopted as part of the base broadening in the 1986 Tax Reform Act; the 1997 legislation increased these limits and introduced Roth IRAs. All but the very high income individuals and couples now have access to IRAs.

There has been considerable debate among economists about the effect of IRAs on savings. Some statistical studies have found powerful savings effects of IRAs and have argued that advertising of the tax benefit has caused people to save. Others have disputed the evidence from those studies and argued that there is no historical evidence of an IRA savings effect, and that economic theory does not support such an effect. Still others have argued that IRAs are less important in increasing overall savings than the more generous thrift savings accounts (e.g., 401(k) plans) provided through employers.

Although the dollar contribution ceilings and income limits on IRAs keep the provision from providing benefits to very high income individuals, IRAs do generally benefit well-off individuals who are more likely to save.[4]

The evidence that lower taxes on the return to investments increase savings in general is mixed. Income and substitution effects, which in the one case lower and the other case raise savings, may net out to little or no effect, and most simple evidence suggests that savings rates do not change very much as tax rules change (although there has been a trend downward in private savings rates).

## End Notes

[1] See Joint Committee on Taxation, *Estimates of Federal Tax Expenditures for 2007-2011*, JCS-3-07, Washington, DC, U.S. Government Printing Office, September 24, 2007.

[2] For itemizers, such contributions would be deductible, so the provision would not matter for them. It would matter for non-itemizers, and also because there are some limits on itemizwed deducitons for very large contributions relative to income. It could also affect the taxation of social security benefits, which are determined by adjusted gross income.

[3] See CRS Report RL32228, *Proposed Savings Accounts: Economic and Budgetary Effects*, by Jane G. Gravelle and Maxim Shvedov, for an economic analysis of this proposal.

[4] See CRS Report RL30255, *Individual Retirement Accounts (IRAs): Issues and Proposed Expansion*, by Thomas L. Hunger for Jane G. Gravelle for further discussion of savings and distributional effects of IRAs.

In: The Role of Savings and Other Issues… ISBN: 978-1-60741-446-9
Editor: Joel K. Harris 

*Chapter 3*

# INCOME AND POVERTY AMONG OLDER AMERICANS IN 2007*

*Patrick Purcell*

## SUMMARY

Older Americans are an economically diverse group. In 2007, the median income of individuals aged 65 and older was $17,382 but incomes varied widely around this average. One-fourth of Americans 65 or older had incomes of less than $10,722 in 2007, while another one-fourth had incomes of $32,160 or more. As Congress considers reforms to Social Security and the laws governing pensions and retirement savings plans, it may be helpful to examine how changes to one income source would affect each of the others, and thus the total income of older Americans.

Older persons receive income from a variety of sources, including earnings, pensions, personal savings, and public programs such as Social Security and Supplemental Security Income. Using data from the March 2008 *Current Population Survey*, this chapter describes the number of elderly individuals and households receiving income from each of these sources and the distribution of income across individuals and households.

* This is an edited, reformatted and augmented version of a CRS Report for Congress publication dated October 2008.

Retirement benefits from Social Security and pensions are the most common sources of income among the aged. In 2007, Social Security paid benefits to 86% of individuals aged 65 and older and to 89% of households in which the householder or the householder's spouse was 65 or older. Social Security is also the largest single source of income among the aged. Sixty-nine percent of Social Security beneficiaries aged 65 or older received more than half of their income from Social Security in 2007. For 41% of elderly recipients and 29% of elderly households, Social Security accounted for more than 90% of total income in 2007. One-third of people aged 65 and older, and fewer than one-half of elderly households, received income from a private or public pension in 2007. Among individuals aged 65 or older who reported income from a government pension, median pension income was $16,629. Among recipients of private pensions, the median pension received in 2007 was just $7,200.

Many Americans prepare for retirement by saving and investing some of their income while they are working. Of the 36.8 million Americans aged 65 and older who were living in households in 2007, 18.9 million (5 1%) received income from assets, such as interest, dividends, rent, and royalties. Most received small amounts of income from the assets they owned. Of individuals aged 65 or older who received income from assets in 2007, half received less than $1,585. Of households with a householder or spouse aged 65 or older, 57% percent received income from assets in 2007. Among these households, median income from assets in 2007 was $2,254.

Earnings are an important source of income for older Americans, especially those under age 70. Although there was a trend toward earlier retirement from about 1960 to 1985, over the past 20 years more Americans have continued to work at older ages. In 2007, median earnings of individuals aged 55 to 64 who worked were $37,000, while the median earnings of workers aged 65 to 69 were $25,000. Among all workers 65 and older, median earnings in 2007 were $20,000. Poverty among those aged 65 and older has fallen from one in three older persons in 1960 to less than one in ten today. Although the overall rate of poverty is relatively low, it remains high for women, minorities, the less-educated, and people over age 80.

## INTRODUCTION

This chapter describes the income and poverty status of the 36.8 million Americans aged 65 and older who were living in households in 2007.[1] Older persons receive income from a variety of sources, including earnings, pensions, personal savings, and public programs such as Social Security and Supplemental Security Income. The substantial variation in the number of people receiving income from each source and the amounts they receive from each source are the main topics of this chapter. Using data from the March 2008 *Current Population Survey*, this chapter describes the number of elderly individuals and households receiving income from earnings, pensions, Social Security, assets, veterans' benefits, public assistance, and other sources. It also describes how the proportion of total income received from each source differs between high-income individuals and households and low-income individuals and households.

In addition to looking at sources and amounts of income, the report examines the income of the elderly relative to the federal poverty thresholds. In 2007, 9.7% of Americans 65 and older had family incomes below the federal poverty thresholds of $9,944 for a single person and $12,550 for a couple. The 2007 poverty rate for Americans 65 and older was lower than both the poverty rate for the population 18 to 64 years old (10.9%) and the poverty rate among children under age 18 (1 8.0%).[2]

Although income is an important measure of a person's economic well-being, it is not the only such measure, nor is it always the best one. Individuals with the same cash income may have significantly different levels of financial assets or other forms of wealth. Some own their own homes while others rent. Some receive non- cash benefits from their former employers, such as fully or partially paid health insurance, while others have to pay for health services or insurance out-of-pocket. The federal and state governments also provide many non-cash benefits and services such as Medicaid, Food Stamps, and the Low-Income Home Energy Assistance Program that improve the financial circumstances of lower-income families, but which do not show up in measures of cash income. Finally, some older Americans live with family members or receive considerable non-financial assistance from their families, while others live alone and pay someone to perform household chores or to provide personal care services. Even with these limitations, however, the amount of income that older Americans receive is an important measure of their ability to purchase the goods and services that contribute to their economic well-being.

## The Data

The findings in this chapter are based on data collected in the March 2008 *Current Population Survey* (CPS), conducted by the Bureau of the Census. The March 2008 CPS consisted of interviews with approximately 75,900 households, comprising a representative sample of the civilian, non-institutionalized population of the United States. Each March, the survey includes detailed questions on sources and amounts of income received during the previous calendar year. The CPS is widely used by researchers in government, academia, and the private sector, and it is the source of the official statistics published annually by the Census Bureau on median family income, the number of Americans living in poverty, and the number of people without health insurance. Like any survey, the CPS is subject to error. *Sampling error* occurs if the households selected to participate in the survey are not representative of the population. *Non-sampling error* occurs if survey participants provide inaccurate information or if their responses are incorrectly recorded.

## INDIVIDUAL INCOME AND HOUSEHOLD INCOME

Income figures in this chapter are shown both for individual persons and for households. Individuals are classified by the individual's age. One-person households are classified according to the age of the householder. Married-couple households are classified by the age of the older of the householder or the householder's spouse. This differs from the Census Bureau's methodology, which classifies households by the age of the householder. The methodology adopted by CRS has the advantage of including in the count of elderly households all households in which *either* the householder or the householder's spouse is 65 or older. The number of persons in poverty is based on the Census Bureau's poverty thresholds, the family's income, and the number of persons in the family.[3]

## MEDIAN INDIVIDUAL AND HOUSEHOLD INCOME

In 2007, 96.5% of individuals aged 65 and older had income from one or more sources. The median total income of these individuals was $17,382. (See **Table 1**.) Of all households in which either the householder or the householder's spouse (if present) was 65 or older, 98.9% had income from one or more sources, and the median income of these households was $29,730. (See **Table 2**.) In general, because more than one member of a household may have income from one or more sources, elderly households were more likely to have income from each source, and had greater income from each source, than elderly individuals. For example, 34.7% of households in which the householder or householder's spouse was 65 or older had income from earnings, and the median earnings of those households were $30,000. In contrast, just 19.7% of individuals aged 65 or older had income from earnings in 2007, and the median earned income of these individuals was $20,000. Because most individuals aged 65 and older receive Social Security, the proportion of elderly households that had income from Social Security in 2007 was only slightly higher than the percentage of elderly individuals with Social Security income. Eighty-nine percent of households in which the householder or householder's spouse was 65 or older had income from Social Security, as did 86% of individuals aged 65 or older. However, the median Social Security income of elderly households that received Social Security was 26% greater than the Social Security income of individual recipients. Median household Social Security income was $15,012, while median individual Social Security income was $11,922.

Elderly households also were more likely than elderly individuals to have received income from private pensions, public pensions, and assets. In 2007, 14.5% of households in which the householder or householder's spouse was 65 or older received income from public-sector pensions, compared to 10.9% of individuals aged 65 and older. Elderly households with public-sector pension income had median pension income of $17,400, compared to $16,629 among elderly individuals with public pension income. Thirty percent of households in which the householder or householder's spouse was 65 or older received income from private-sector pensions, compared to 23% of individuals aged 65 and older. Elderly households with private-sector pension income had median pension income of $8,052, compared to $7,200 among elderly individuals with private pension income. Fifty-seven percent of elderly households had income from assets (mainly interest, dividends, and rent) in

2007 compared to 53.5% of individuals aged 65 and older. Among elderly households with asset income, the median amount of asset income was $2,254, whereas among elderly individuals with asset income, the median amount of asset income was $1,585.

Relatively few elderly individuals and households received income from veterans' benefits, public assistance, or other income sources in 2007. Just 3.8% of elderly households and 2.7% of elderly individuals received income from veterans' benefits, which consist mainly of veteran's compensation for service-related disabilities and veterans' pensions for indigent elderly veterans. Among elderly households that received income from veterans' programs, the median amount received in 2007 was $9,000; among elderly individuals with income from veterans' benefits, the median amount received in 2007 was $8,400.

**Table 1. Percentage of Older Individuals with Income in 2007, Mean and Median Amounts, by Source**

| | Age | | | | | |
|---|---|---|---|---|---|---|
| | **Total, 55+** | **55 to 64** | **Total, 65+** | **65 to 69** | **70 to 79** | **80+** |
| **Total individuals (in thousands)** | **70,092** | **33,302** | **36,790** | **11,165** | **15,776** | **9,849** |
| **Percentage reporting no income** | **5.0** | **6.5** | **3.5** | **3.7** | **3.6** | **3.3** |
| **Total income** | | | | | | |
| Percentage with any income | 95.0 | 93.5 | 96.5 | 96.3 | 96.4 | 96.7 |
| Mean total income ($) | 36,754 | 46,223 | 28,449 | 35,823 | 26,627 | 23,033 |
| Median total income ($) | 22,800 | 33,000 | 17,382 | 21,841 | 16,722 | 15,648 |
| **Earnings** | | | | | | |
| Percentage with earnings | 42.8 | 68.4 | 19.7 | 35.1 | 17.3 | 6.0 |
| Mean earnings ($) | 46,088 | 49,422 | 35,591 | 39,485 | 29,849 | 36,225 |
| Median earnings ($) | 33,000 | 37,000 | 20,000 | 25,000 | 15,600 | 18,200 |
| **Social Security** | | | | | | |
| Percentage with Social Security | 53.0 | 16.8 | 85.8 | 78.1 | 88.5 | 90.1 |
| Mean Social Security ($) | 12,014 | 11,425 | 12,119 | 12,273 | 11,934 | 12,260 |
| Median Social Security ($) | 11,802 | 10,722 | 11,922 | 11,922 | 11,802 | 11,922 |
| **Public pensions** | | | | | | |
| Percentage with public | 8.7 | 6.4 | 10.9 | 10.9 | 11.0 | 10.6 |

| | Total, 55+ | 55 to 64 | Total, 65+ | 65 to 69 | 70 to 79 | 80+ |
|---|---|---|---|---|---|---|
| pensions | | | | | | |
| Mean public pension ($) | 23,531 | 26,445 | 21,991 | 25,231 | 21,904 | 18,358 |
| Median public pension ($) | 18,000 | 22,000 | 16,629 | 19,200 | 17,000 | 14,400 |
| | Age | | | | | |
| | Total, 55+ | 55 to 64 | Total, 65+ | 65 to 69 | 70 to 79 | 80+ |
| **Private pensions or annuities** | | | | | | |
| Percentage with private pensions | 15.9 | 8.3 | 22.8 | 19.6 | 23.7 | 24.8 |
| Mean private pension ($) | 12,809 | 16,475 | 11,605 | 14,137 | 11,088 | 10,135 |
| Median private pension ($) | 8,388 | 12,000 | 7,200 | 9,500 | 7,200 | 6,288 |
| **Income from assets** | | | | | | |
| Percentage with asset income | 52.4 | 53.5 | 51.3 | 52.3 | 51.8 | 49.7 |
| Mean asset income ($) | 7,366 | 6,413 | 8,265 | 9,120 | 8,128 | 7,473 |
| Median asset income ($) | 1,301 | 1,011 | 1,585 | 1,601 | 1,800 | 1,375 |
| **Veterans' benefits** | | | | | | |
| Percentage with veterans' benefits | 2.5 | 2.4 | 2.7 | 2.1 | 2.2 | 4.1 |
| Mean veterans' benefit ($) | 11,880 | 12,579 | 11,322 | 11,558 | 12,494 | 10,160 |
| Median veterans' benefit ($) | 8,532 | 8,544 | 8,400 | 8,532 | 10,248 | 6,480 |
| **Public assistance**[a] | | | | | | |
| Percentage with public assistance | 3.2 | 3.2 | 3.3 | 3.3 | 3.0 | 3.5 |
| Mean public assistance ($) | 6,174 | 7,105 | 5,335 | 5,650 | 5,108 | 5,311 |
| Median public assistance ($) | 6,120 | 7,440 | 4,776 | 4,800 | 4,416 | 4,800 |
| **Other income**[b] | | | | | | |
| Percentage with other income | 4.2 | 5.4 | 3.2 | 3.5 | 3.2 | 2.8 |
| Mean other income ($) | 8,421 | 8,319 | 8,576 | 9,010 | 8,255 | 8,550 |
| Median other income ($) | 4,344 | 4,400 | 4,000 | 3,588 | 3,984 | 4,800 |

Source: Congressional Research Service (CRS) analysis of the March 2008 *Current Population Survey*.

a. Includes Supplemental Security Income, Temporary Assistance for Needy Families, and state general assistance.

b. Includes unemployment compensation, workers' compensation, and income from unidentified sources.

In 2007, 4.8% of elderly households and 3.3% of elderly individuals received income from public assistance, which consists mainly of Supplemental Security Income, Temporary Assistance for Needy Families, and state general assistance. Among elderly households that received income from public assistance programs, the median amount received in 2007 was $5,376; among elderly individuals with income from public assistance, the median amount received in 2007 was $4,776.

**Table 2. Percentage of Older Households with Income in 2007, Mean and Median Amounts, by Source**

| | Age | | | | | |
|---|---|---|---|---|---|---|
| | **Total, 55+** | **55 to 64** | **Total, 65+** | **65 to 69** | **70 to 79** | **80+** |
| **Total households (in thousands)** | **46,185** | **20,702** | **25,483** | **7,164** | **10,847** | **7,472** |
| **Percentage reporting no income** | **1.2** | **1.2** | **1.1** | **1.1** | **1.1** | **1.1** |
| **Total income** | | | | | | |
| Percentage with any income | 98.8 | 98.8 | 98.9 | 98.9 | 98.9 | 98.9 |
| Mean total income ($) | 61,393 | 79,521 | 46,682 | 62,193 | 45,365 | 33,719 |
| Median total income ($) | 40,689 | 60,491 | 29,730 | 42,214 | 30,522 | 21,928 |
| **Earnings** | | | | | | |
| Percentage with earnings | 56.4 | 83.1 | 34.7 | 56.2 | 33.7 | 15.4 |
| Mean earnings ($) | 66,262 | 76,455 | 46,417 | 54,967 | 39,135 | 39,679 |
| Median earnings ($) | 49,000 | 60,000 | 30,000 | 38,000 | 25,000 | 24,513 |
| **Social Security** | | | | | | |
| Percentage with Social Security | 59.0 | 22.4 | 88.8 | 80.4 | 91.5 | 92.9 |
| Mean Social Security ($) | 16,017 | 13,513 | 16,530 | 16,362 | 17,265 | 15,619 |
| Median Social Security ($) | 14,400 | 12,072 | 15,012 | 15,282 | 15,600 | 14,022 |
| **Public pensions** | | | | | | |
| Percentage with public pensions | 12.0 | 8.8 | 14.5 | 14.5 | 15.5 | 13.2 |
| Mean public pension ($) | 25,778 | 29,260 | 24,054 | 27,139 | 24,704 | 19,706 |
| Median public pension ($) | 19,960 | 24,000 | 17,400 | 19,800 | 19,200 | 14,400 |

| | Age | | | | | |
|---|---|---|---|---|---|---|
| | Total, 55+ | 55 to 64 | Total, 65+ | 65 to 69 | 70 to 79 | 80+ |
| **Private pensions or annuities** | | | | | | |
| Percentage with private pensions | 22.1 | 12.1 | 30.2 | 27.1 | 32.1 | 30.7 |
| Mean private pension ($) | 13,895 | 17,362 | 12,771 | 15,461 | 12,520 | 10,877 |
| Median private pension ($) | 8,940 | 12,000 | 8,052 | 10,000 | 8,272 | 6,900 |
| **Income from assets** | | | | | | |
| Percentage with asset income | 57.8 | 59.0 | 56.8 | 57.0 | 57.4 | 55.8 |
| Mean asset income ($) | 10,639 | 9,184 | 11,869 | 13,970 | 11,826 | 9,871 |
| Median asset income ($) | 2,000 | 1,600 | 2,254 | 2,400 | 2,490 | 1,928 |
| **Veterans' benefits** | | | | | | |
| Percentage with veterans' benefits | 3.8 | 3.7 | 3.8 | 3.5 | 3.3 | 5.0 |
| Mean veterans' benefit ($) | 12,147 | 12,866 | 11,579 | 11,238 | 12,583 | 10,841 |
| Median veterans' benefit ($) | 8,544 | 8,400 | 9,000 | 7,200 | 10,248 | 7,740 |
| **Public assistance**[a] | | | | | | |
| Percentage with public assistance | 5.1 | 5.6 | 4.8 | 4.9 | 4.9 | 4.5 |
| Mean public assistance ($) | 6,748 | 7,362 | 6,163 | 6,452 | 5,984 | 6,144 |
| Median public assistance ($) | 6,600 | 7,284 | 5,376 | 5,400 | 4,800 | 6,000 |
| **Other income**[b] | | | | | | |
| Percentage with other income | 7.4 | 9.9 | 5.4 | 6.6 | 5.3 | 4.5 |
| Mean other income ($) | 8,346 | 7,810 | 9,144 | 9,437 | 8,714 | 9,467 |
| Median other income ($) | 4,480 | 4,344 | 4,800 | 4,140 | 4,200 | 6,000 |

Source: Congressional Research Service (CRS) analysis of the March 2008 *Current Population Survey*.

Note: Households are grouped according to the age of the older of the householder or householder's spouse.

a. Includes Supplemental Security Income, Temporary Assistance for Needy Families, and state general assistance.

b. Includes unemployment compensation, workers' compensation, and income from unidentified sources.

In 2007, 5.4% of elderly households and 3.2% of elderly individuals received income from other sources, including unemployment compensation, workers' compensation, and other unidentified sources. Among elderly households that received income from these sources, the median amount received in 2007 was $4,800; among elderly individuals with income from other sources, the median amount received in 2007 was $4,000.

## SOURCES OF INCOME BY INCOME QUARTILE

**Figures 1** through **4** show the percentage of total income from each source received by all individuals aged 65 and older with any income in 2007. For example, **Figure 1** shows that among individuals with total income in the highest 25% among all persons aged 65 and older — those with 2007 income of more than $32,160 — 37% of total income came from earnings, 21% of income came from pensions, 21% of income came from assets, 19% of income came from Social Security, less than 1% of income came from public assistance, and 2% came from other sources. Thus, among elderly individuals in the highest income quartile, 79% of total income came from earnings, pensions, and assets.

In contrast, among elderly individuals whose income in 2007 was in the lowest income quartile for people 65 and older — those with income of less than $10,722 — 2% of all income came from earnings, 3% of income came from pensions, 4% of income came from assets, 84% of income came from Social Security, 6% came from public assistance, and 1% came from other sources. (See **Figure 4**.) Among individuals in the lowest income quartile, just 9% of total income came from earnings, pensions, and assets. **Figure 2** and **Figure 3** show that Social Security comprised 55% and 83%, respectively, of income received by individuals aged 65 and older in the second and third income quartiles in 2007.

**Figures 5** through 8 show the percentage of total income from each source received by all elderly households with any income in 2007. For example, **Figure 5** shows that among elderly households with total income in the highest 25% among all households in which either the householder or householder's spouse was 65 or older — those with 2007 income of more than $56,973 — 47% of all income came from earnings, 15% of income came from pensions, 20% of income came from assets, 16% of income came from Social Security, less than 1% of income came from public assistance, and 2% came from other sources. Thus, among elderly households in the highest income quartile, 82% of total income came from earnings, pensions, and assets.

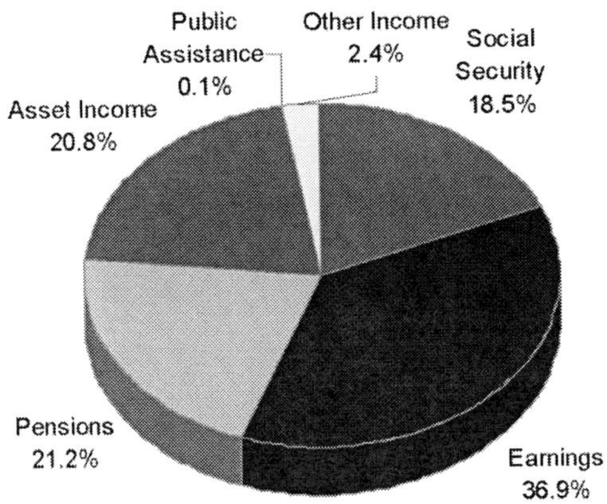


Figure 1. Sources of Individual Income, Top Quartile, Age 65+.
2007 Individual Income of More Than $32,160.

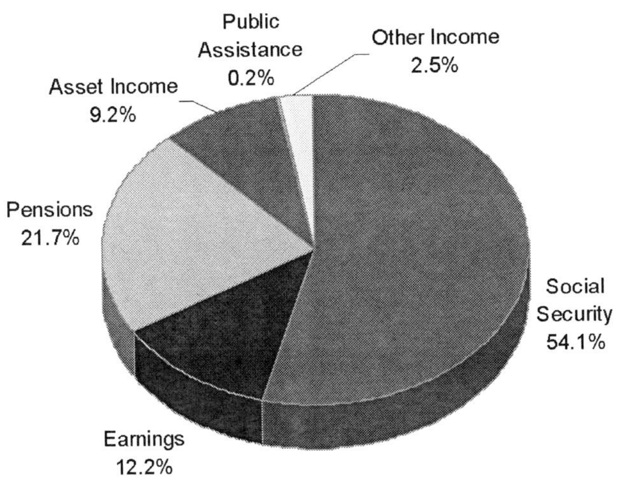


Source: Both figures from CRS analysis of the March 2008 *Current Population Survey*.

Figure 2. Sources of Individual Income, Second Quartile, Age 65+
2007 Individual Income of $17,382 to $32,160.

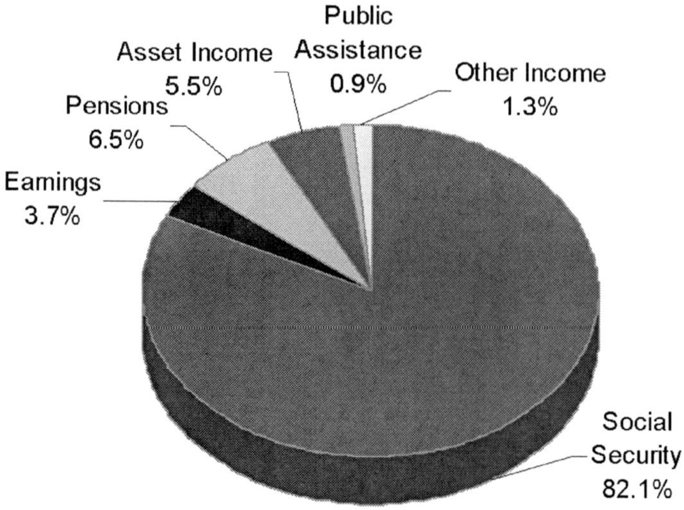


Figure 3. Sources of Individual Income, Third Quartile, Age 65+
2007 Individual Income of $10,722 to $17,382.

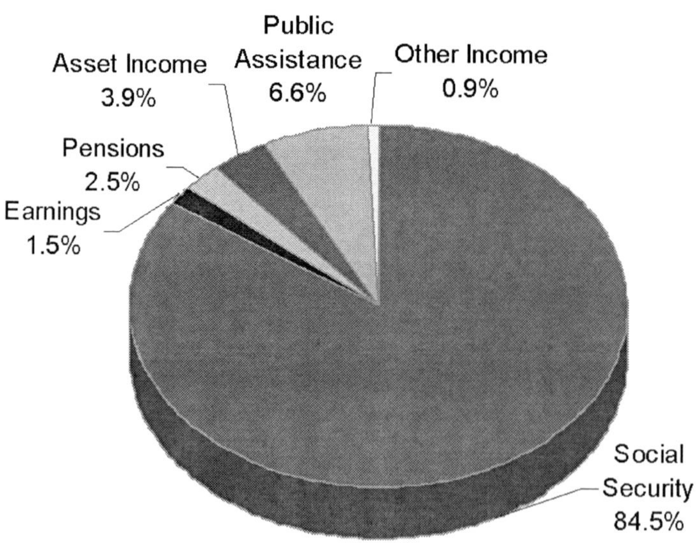


Source: Both figures from CRS analysis of the March 2008 *Current Population Survey.*

Figure 4. Sources of Individual Income, Bottom Quartile, Age 65+
2007 Individual Income of Less Than $10,722.

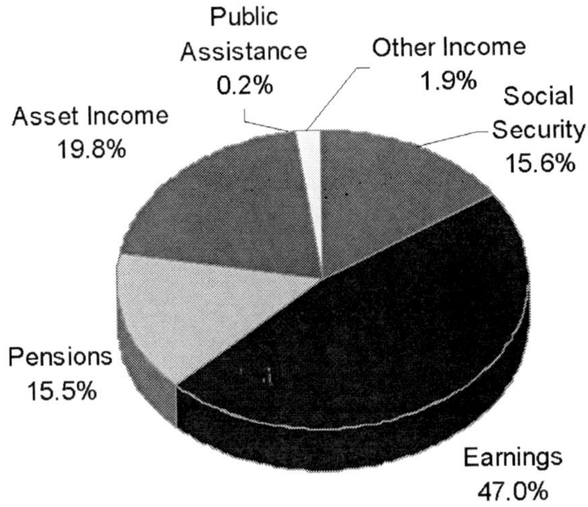


Figure 5. Sources of Household Income, Top Quartile, Age 65+
2007 Household Income of More Than $56,973.

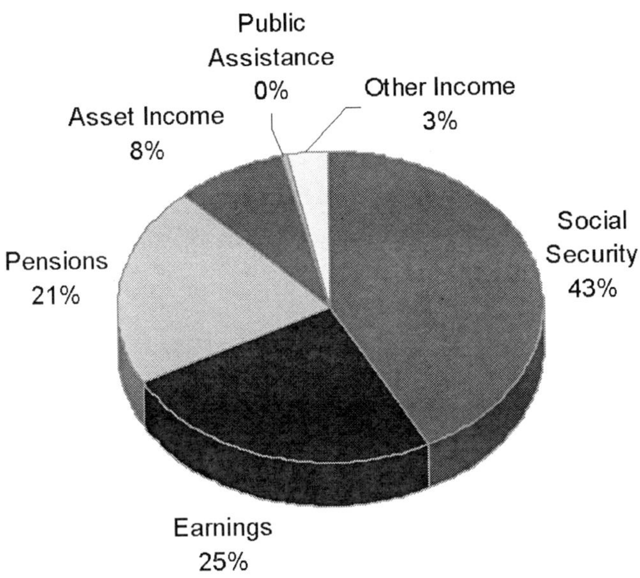


Source: Both figures from CRS analysis of the March 2008 *Current Population Survey*.

Figure 6. Sources of Household Income, Second Quartile, Age 65+
2007 Household Income of $29,730 to $56,973.

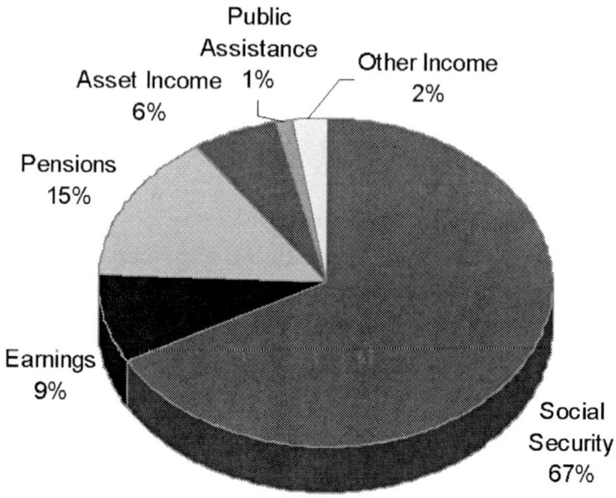


Figure 7. Sources of Household Income, Third Quartile, Age 65+
2007 Household Income of $16,244 to $29,730.

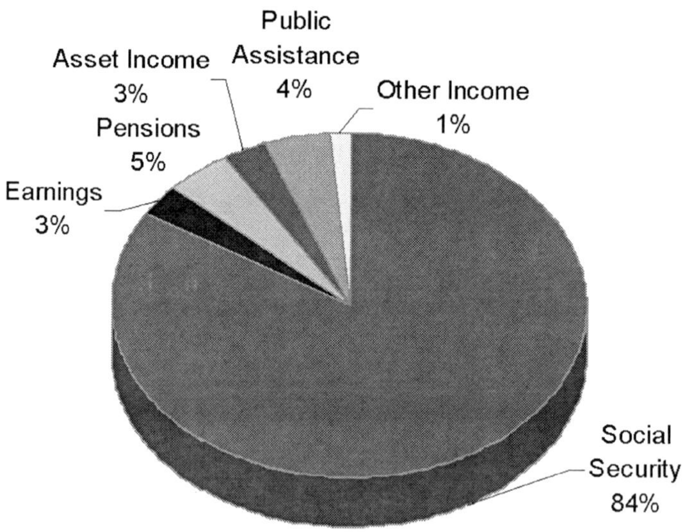


Source: Both figures from CRS analysis of the March 2008 *Current Population Survey*.

Figure 8. Sources of Household Income, Bottom Quartile, Age 65+
2007 Household Income of Less Than $16,244.

In contrast, among elderly households whose income in 2007 was in the lowest income quartile for households in which the householder or spouse was 65 or older — those with income of less than $16,244 — 3% of all income came from earnings, 5% of income came from pensions, 3% of income came from assets, 84% of income came from Social Security, 4% came from public assistance, and 1% came from other sources. (See **Figure 8**.) Among households in the lowest income quartile, 11% of total income came from earnings, pensions, and assets. **Figure 6** and **Figure 7** show that Social Security comprised 43% and 67%, respectively, of income received by elderly households in the second and third income quartiles in 2007.

## Median Individual and Household Income by Demographic Characteristics

Income received by the elderly varies significantly by age, sex, race, education and marital status. **Figure 9** shows that in 2007, individuals between the ages of 65 and 69 had a median income of $21,841 while those who were 80 or older had a median income of $15,648. Men 65 and older had a median income of $24,142, while women 65 and older had a median income of $13,877. The median income of older African Americans, $13,104, was 71% of the median income of older white Americans — $18,537. The median income of older Americans increases substantially with their educational level. Those without high-school diplomas had a median income of $12,200 in 2007, whereas college graduates had a median income of $34,593. The median income of married individuals aged 65 and older — $18,448 — was $2,026 higher than the median income of single individuals aged 65 and older.

**Figure 10** shows the median income of households in which either the householder or the householder's spouse was aged 65 or older.[4] In 2007, the median income of households in which the householder was between the ages of 65 and 69 was $43,159. Households in which the householder was 80 or older had a median income of $20,995. Elderly households with a male householder had a median income of $38,222, while households with a female householder had a median income of $23,400. The median income of elderly households in which the householder was African American was $21,184, just 68% of the median income of elderly households with a white householder. Elderly households in which the householder did not have a high-school diploma had a median income of $1 8,230 in 2007, while elderly households headed by a college graduate had a median income of $57,940. The median income of married-couple households with a householder or spouse aged 65 or older was $45,036 in 2007, more than twice the median income of elderly households in which the householder was not married ($19,722).

## INCOME FROM RETIREMENT BENEFITS

### Social Security

Retirement benefits from Social Security are the most common source of income among Americans aged 65 and older. In 2007, Social Security paid benefits to 86% of individuals aged 65 and older and to 89% of households in which the householder or householder's spouse was 65 or older. Social Security is the largest single source of income among the aged. In 2007, 68.5% of Social Security beneficiaries aged 65 or older received more than half of their income from Social Security, and 5 9.3% of elderly households that received Social Security benefits received more than half of their total household income from Social Security. (See **Table 3** and **Table 4**.)

For 40.6% of elderly individual recipients, Social Security accounted for more than 90% of their income in 2007. Among elderly households receiving Social Security, 29% received 90% or more of their total household income from Social Security. Although Social Security is an important source of income for a majority of the elderly, the benefit amounts paid by Social Security are relatively small compared with many recipients' pre-retirement incomes. According to the Social Security Administration, Social Security retired worker benefits replace approximately 55% of the earnings of a career-long low-wage earner, 41% of the earnings of a career-long average-wage earner, and 27% of the earnings of a career- long high-wage earner.

Average monthly Social Security benefits in 2008 are $1,079 for a retired worker and $1,761 for an elderly couple. As **Figure 11** shows, 37% of all individual beneficiaries received less than $10,000 from Social Security in 2007, and just 7% received more than $20,000 in Social Security benefits. Because many elderly households have more than one beneficiary, the amount of Social Security benefits received by households with at least one beneficiary is higher than the amount received by individual recipients. In 2007, 20% of elderly beneficiary households received less than $10,000 from

Social Security, while 30% of households received Social Security benefits totaling more than $20,000. (See **Figure 12**.)

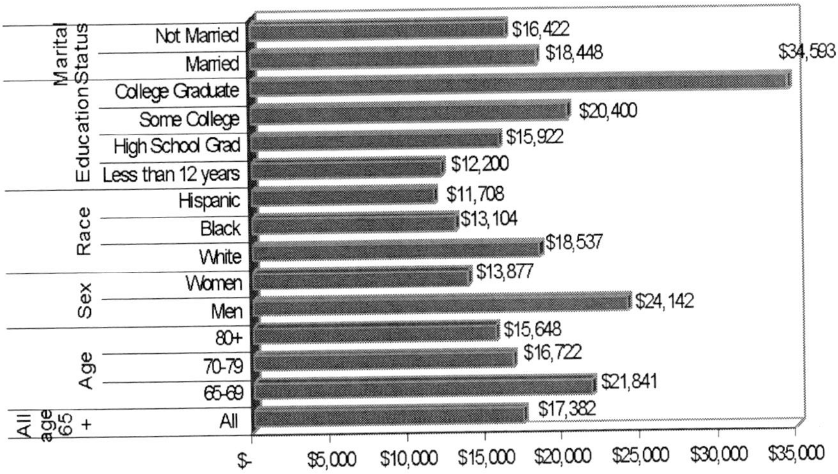


Figure 9. Median Individual Income by Demographic Traits, 2007

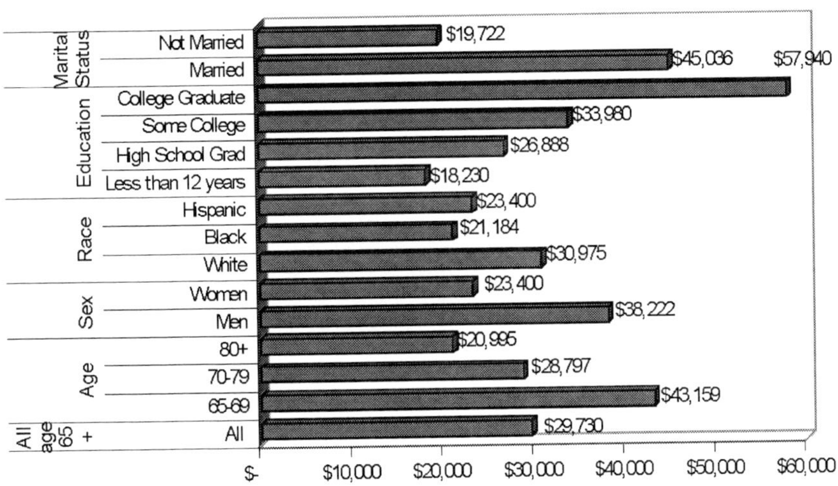


Source: Both figures from CRS analysis of the March 2008 *Current Population Survey*.

Figure 10. Median Household Income by Demographic Traits of Householder, 2007

**Table 3. Social Security as a Percentage of Individual Income among Recipients Aged 65 and Older in 2007**

| Percent of Income from Social Security | Recipients (thousands) | Percent of Recipients |
|---|---|---|
| Less than 10% | 894 | 2.8 |
| 10% to 19% | 2,057 | 6.5 |
| 20% to 29% | 2,138 | 6.8 |
| 30% to 39% | 2,289 | 7.2 |
| 40% to 49% | 2,574 | 8.2 |
| 50% to 59% | 2,487 | 7.9 |
| 60% to 69% | 2,150 | 6.8 |
| 70% to 79% | 1,992 | 6.3 |
| 80% to 89% | 2,162 | 6.9 |
| 90% to 99% | 3,992 | 12.6 |
| 100% of income | 8,820 | 28.0 |

Source: CRS analysis of the March 2008 *Current Population Survey*.

Note: In 2007, 31.6 million people aged 65 or older received income from Social Security, and 5.2 million elderly people had no Social Security income.

**Table 4. Social Security as a Percentage of Household Income among Recipient Households of Those Aged 65 and Older in 2007**

| Percent of Income from Social Security | Households (thousands) | Percent of Households |
|---|---|---|
| Less than 10% | 799 | 3.7 |
| 10% to 19% | 2,044 | 9.5 |
| 20% to 29% | 2,054 | 9.5 |
| 30% to 39% | 1,965 | 9.1 |
| 40% to 49% | 1,919 | 8.9 |
| 50% to 59% | 1,943 | 9.0 |
| 60% to 69% | 1,742 | 8.0 |
| 70% to 79% | 1,477 | 6.8 |
| 80% to 89% | 1,466 | 6.8 |
| 90% to 99% | 2,260 | 10.5 |
| 100% of income | 3,932 | 18.2 |

Source: CRS analysis of the March 2008 *Current Population Survey*.

Note: In 2007, 21.6 million households in which the householder or the household's spouse was 65 or older received Social Security, and 3.9 million elderly households had no Social Security income.

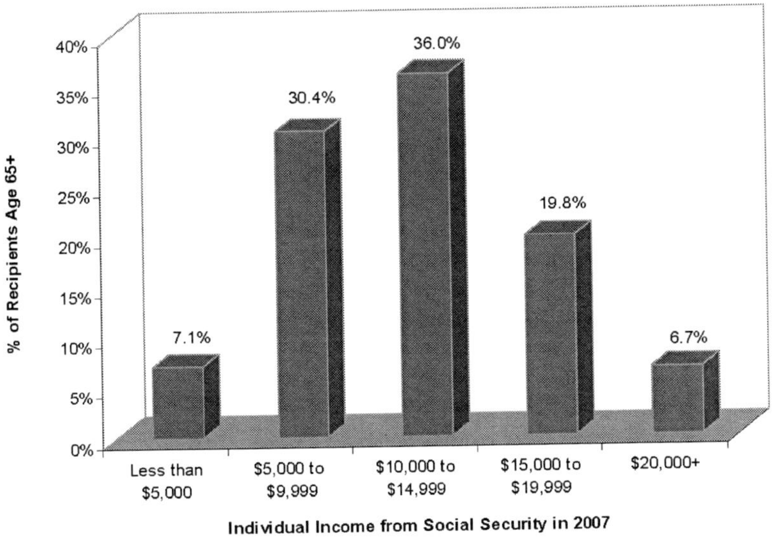


Figure 11. Social Security Income of Individuals Aged 65+, 2007.

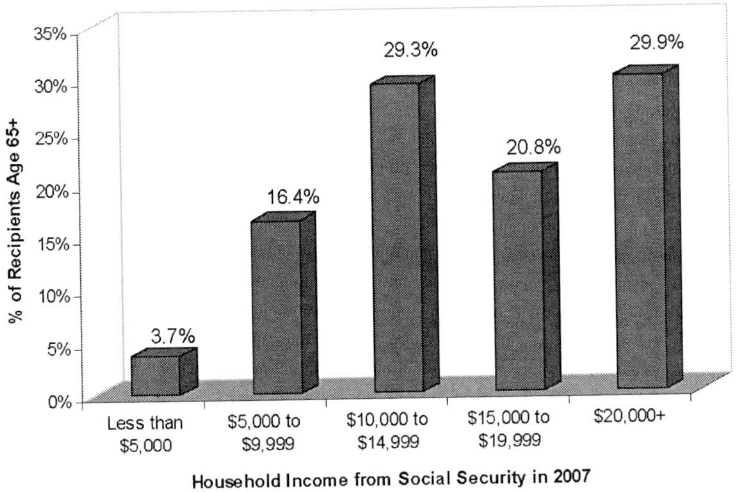


Source: CRS analysis of the March 2008 *Current Population Survey.*

Figure 12. Social Security Income of Households Aged 65+, 2007

## Pension Income

Since the late 1970s, the proportion of American workers who participate in employer-sponsored retirement plans has remained fairly stable at about half of the workforce. The Department of Labor's *National Compensation Survey* reports that in March 2008, 51% of all private-sector workers participated in an employer- sponsored retirement plan of some kind. However, a point-in-time snapshot of pension participation is a poor indicator of who will receive pension income in retirement. Some workers not covered by a pension plan today may have earned a pension at a previous job, or they may earn a pension benefit in the future. Others who are currently participating in a pension plan may never fully vest in their pension benefit, or they might take their accrued benefit as a lump sum before retirement and spend all or part of the distribution.

To receive pension income in retirement, an individual must remain a participant in the plan long enough to earn a pension benefit and must not spend the accrued benefit before retirement. In 1986, Congress shortened the maximum vesting period (the length of time it takes to earn a pension benefit) from 10 years to 5 years, thus making it easier for employees whose employer sponsors a pension to earn a benefit under the plan.[5] On the other hand, many employers offer separating employees the opportunity to take their accrued retirement benefit as a lump-sum distribution. Most defined contribution plans, such as those authorized under §401(k) of the Internal Revenue Code, and some defined benefit plans permit departing employees to take a lump-sum distribution. Many employees roll these distributions into another employer-sponsored retirement plan or into an individual retirement account, but some spend all or part of the distribution, thus reducing their future retirement income.[6]

In 2007, 12.1 million people aged 65 and older — 34.7% of that age group — received income from a private or public pension.[7] Of these people, 4.0 million had income from a public-sector pension — that is, from previous employment in the federal, state, or local government — and 8.4 million received income from private- sector pension plans.[8] Together, the federal, state, and local governments account for only about one-seventh of all jobs in the United States. In 2007, for example, just 14% of all workers in the United States were employed by the federal, state, and local governments. Nevertheless, *one-third* of pension recipients aged 65 and older received income from government-sponsored pension plans in 2007.

The disparity between the percentage of jobs that are in the government sector and the percentage of retirees with government pensions is accounted for mainly by two factors, both of which make it more likely that a government employee will earn a pension benefit than will a worker in the private sector. First, more government jobs than private-sector jobs offer pension benefits to their employees. According to the Department of Labor, in March 2008, 89% of state and local government employees worked at jobs that offered retirement benefits, compared to 61% of employees in the private sector. Second, government employees tend to stay in their jobs longer than private-sector workers, making it more likely that the government employee will fully vest in the pension benefits he or she has earned. The Department of Labor reports that in January 2008, the median tenure of government workers with their current employer was double the median tenure of workers in the private sector. Public-sector employees had a median tenure of 7.2 years, while private-sector workers had a median tenure of 3.6 years.[9]

Public-sector employees not only are more likely to receive a pension in retirement than are workers in the private-sector; they also receive larger pensions than those who worked in the private sector. Among the 4.0 million people aged 65 and older who reported income from a government pension in 2007, the median annual amount was $16,629. Twenty-nine percent of people receiving a public- sector pension had pension income of less than $10,000 in 2007, while 25% reported pension income of more than $30,000. (See **Figure 13**.) Among the 8.4 million people aged 65 and older who reported income from a private-sector pension in 2007, the median annual amount was $7,200. Sixty percent of private pension recipients reported that their pension income was less than $10,000 in 2007 and 8% reported pension income of more than $30,000.

Among the 3.7 million elderly households that reported income from a government pension in 2007, the median annual amount was $17,400. Twenty-seven percent of households receiving a public-sector pension reported that their pension income was less than $10,000 in 2007; 29% reported pension income of more than $30,000. (See **Figure 14**.) Among the 7.7 million elderly households that reported income from a private-sector pension in 2007, the median annual amount was $8,052. Fifty-seven percent of households with private pension income reported that their pension income was less than $10,000 in 2007, and 10% reported pension income of more than $30,000.

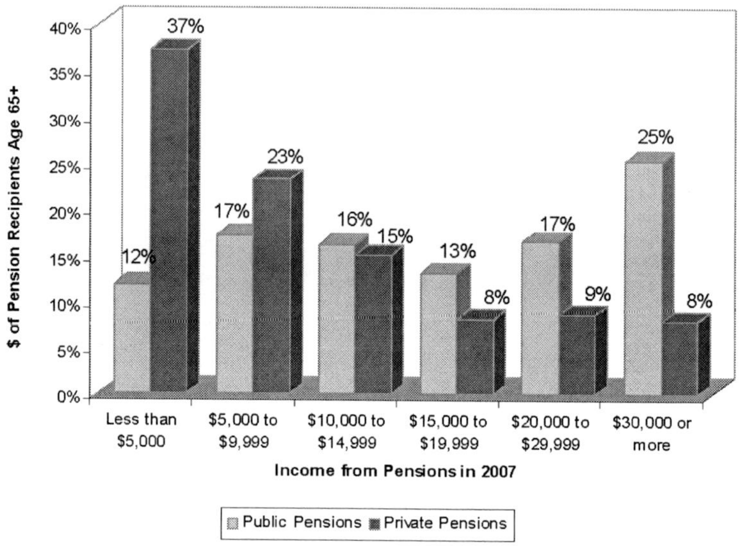


Figure 13. Individual Income from Pensions in 2007

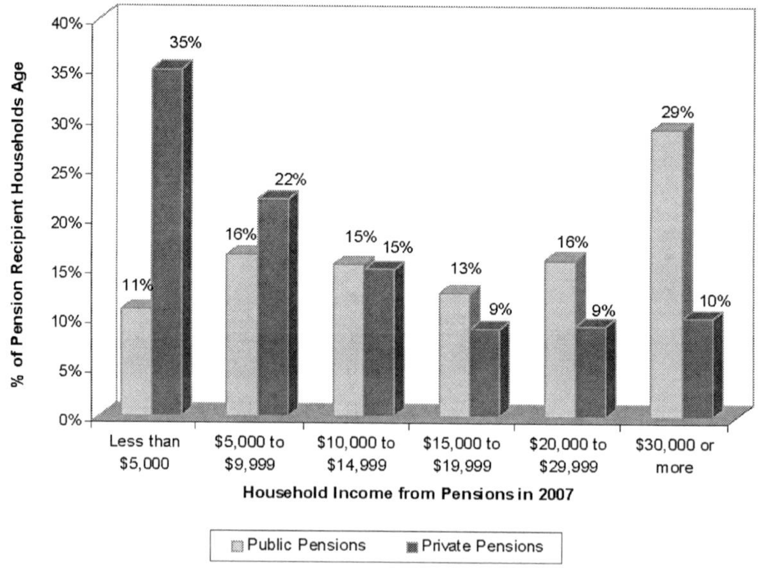


Source: CRS analysis of the March 2008 *Current Population Survey.*

Figure 14. Household Income from Pensions in 2007

## Two Types of Pension Plans

Over the past 25 years, there has been a shift in the distribution of retirement plans and of plan participants from *defined benefit* plans to *defined contribution* plans. A defined benefit or "DB" plan usually pays as a lifelong annuity based on the employee's length of service and average salary. Most DB plans are funded entirely by employer contributions and investment earnings. Defined contribution or "DC" plans are much like savings accounts maintained by employers on behalf of each participating employee. The employer contributes a specific dollar amount or percentage of pay, which is invested in stocks, bonds, or other assets. The employee usually contributes to the plan, too. In a DC plan, it is the employee who bears the investment risk. At retirement, the balance in the account is the sum of all contributions plus interest, dividends, and capital gains — or losses. The account balance is usually distributed as a single lump sum. Many large employers recently have converted their traditional DB pensions to hybrid plans that have characteristics of both DB and DC plans, the most popular of which has been the *cash balance plan*. In a cash balance plan, the benefit is defined in terms of an account balance. The employer makes contributions to the plan and pays interest on the accumulated balance. However, these account balances are merely bookkeeping devices. They are not individual accounts owned by the participants. Legally, therefore, a cash balance plan is a defined benefit plan.

## Income from Assets

Many Americans prepare for retirement by saving and investing some of their income while they are working. Of the 36.8 million Americans aged 65 and older who were living in households in 2007, 18.9 million (51%) received income from assets, such as interest, dividends, rent, and royalties. Most received small amounts. Half of those who had income from assets in 2007 received less than $1,585. The data displayed in **Figure 15** show that low-income individuals were less likely to have received income from assets. Among individuals aged 65 and older whose total income in 2007 was less than $10,000, 30% had asset income. In contrast, of those whose total income was more than $50,000, 83% had asset income.

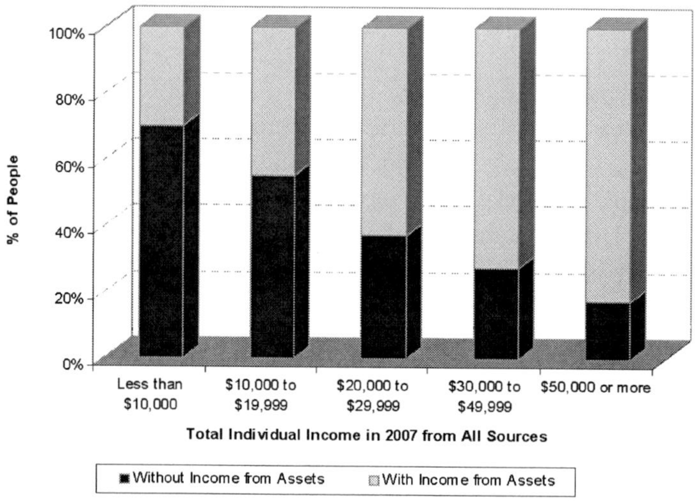


Figure 15. Percentage of Individuals Aged 65 and Older with Income from Assets in 2007, by Total Individual Income

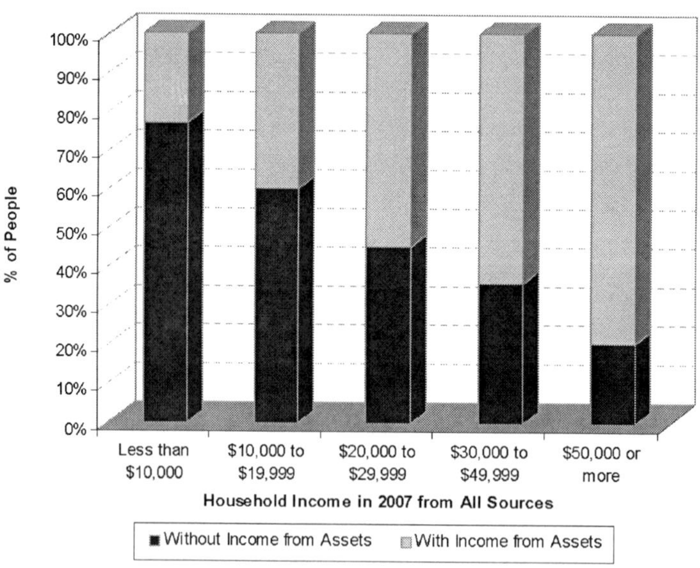


Source: Both figures from CRS analysis of the March 2008 *Current Population Survey.*

Figure 16. Percentage of Households Aged 65 and Older with Income from Assets in 2007, by Total Household Income

Of the 25.5 million households in which either the householder or the householder's spouse was aged 65 or older in 2007, 14.5 million (57%) received income from assets. Most households received relatively small amounts of income from assets. Half of the elderly households that had income from assets in 2007 received less than $2,254. The data displayed in **Figure 16** show that low-income households were less likely to have received income from assets. Among elderly households that had total income in 2007 of less than $10,000, 23% had asset income. On the other hand, of the households with total income of more than $50,000, 79% had asset income.

Median income from assets also differed between the lower-income and higher-income elderly. Among people aged 65 and older with total annual income under $10,000 in 2007, 30% received asset income and the median amount of asset income was only $338. For individuals with total annual incomes of more than $50,000, 83% had asset income, and their median asset income in 2007 was $14,416. (See **Table 5**.) Among households in which the householder or spouse was 65 or older with total annual incomes under $10,000 in 2007, 23% received income from assets, and the median amount of asset income they received was $219. Among elderly households with total annual incomes of more than $50,000, 79% received asset income, and their median asset income in 2007 was $9,000. (See **Table 6**.)

**Table 5. Income from Assets, Individuals 65 and Older, 2007**

| Total Income, 2007 | Number of People (thousands) | Percent with Asset Income | Mean Asset Income | Median Asset Income |
|---|---|---|---|---|
| Less than $10,000 | 7,897 | 29.8 | $888 | $338 |
| $10,000 to $19,999 | 12,184 | 44.6 | 1,947 | 726 |
| $20,000 to $29,999 | 5,647 | 62.6 | 3,726 | 1,799 |
| $30,000 to $39,000 | 3,084 | 71.1 | 5,618 | 2,280 |
| $40,000 to $49,999 | 1,770 | 74.5 | 8,611 | 4,000 |
| $50,000 or more | 4,903 | 82.6 | 26,320 | 14,416 |
| **All persons with any income**[10] | **35,485** | **53.2** | **$8,265** | **$1,585** |

**Table 6. Income from Assets, Households 65 and Older, 2007**

| Total Income, 2007 | Number of Households (thousands) | Percent with Asset Income | Mean Asset Income | Median Asset Income |
|---|---|---|---|---|
| Less than $10,000 | 2,215 | 22.7% | $814 | $219 |
| $10,000 to $19,999 | 6,058 | 39.8 | 1,355 | 400 |
| $20,000 to $29,999 | 4,418 | 54.7 | 2,937 | 1,285 |
| $30,000 to $39,000 | 2,991 | 63.0 | 4,401 | 2,014 |
| $40,000 to $49,999 | 2,133 | 65.4 | 6,116 | 2,844 |
| $50,000 or more | 7,384 | 79.4 | 24,584 | 9,000 |
| **All persons with any income**[11] | **25,199** | **57.4** | **$11,869** | **$2,254** |

Source: Both tables from CRS analysis of the March 2008 *Current Population Survey.*

# EARNED INCOME

Although some people continue to work into their 60s and beyond, labor force participation rates begin to drop after about age 55. Although there was a trend toward earlier retirement from about 1960 to 1985, the trend for the past 20 years has been that more Americans have continued to work at older ages.[12] In March 2008, 73% of men and 63% of women between the ages of 55 and 61 were working either full-time or part-time. Of those between the ages o f 62 and 64, 52% of men and 41% of women were employed. Among 65 to 69-year olds, 33% of men and 26% of women were employed in March 2008. Although the share of older Americans who work declines rapidly after age 65, **Figure 17** shows that 14% of men and 8% of women who were age 70 or older in March 2008 were still working.

Despite the trend to longer working lives, people are progressively less likely to work as they pass age 55 and the average annual earnings of those who continue to work begin to decline at about the same age. This can be attributed to decreases in both wages and the number of hours worked.[13] In 2007, the median earnings of workers aged 55 to 61 were $38,500, while median earnings of workers aged 62 to 64 were $31,000. For those aged 65 or older who were working, median earnings were $20,000 in 2007. **Figure 18** shows the decline in workers' annual earnings as they age. At the top of the earnings scale, 37% of workers aged 55 to 61 earned $50,000 or more in 2007, while only 23% of those aged 65 and older had earned income totaling more than $50,000 in that year. In contrast, while only 9% of Americans aged 55 to 61 who worked in 2007 had total earnings of less than $10,000, 28% of workers aged 65 and older had earnings of $10,000 or less.

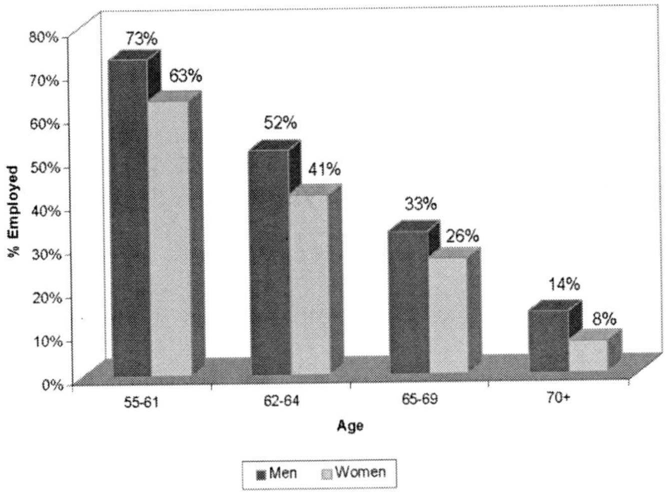


Figure 17. Employment Rates by Age and Sex, March 2008

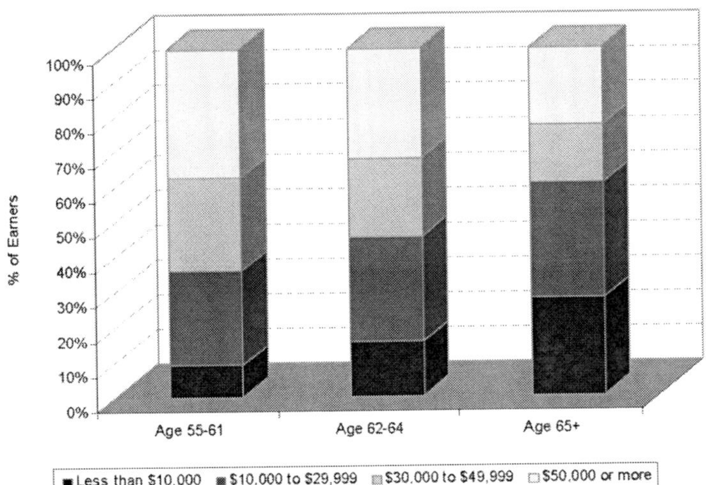


Source: Both figures from CRS analysis of the March 2008 *Current Population Survey.*

Figure 18. Earned Income, by Age, 2007

# POVERTY

Poverty among the elderly has decreased dramatically over the past five decades. In 1959, the poverty rate among Americans aged 65 and older was 35%. Largely due to increases in Social Security benefits, the elderly poverty rate fell to about 15% by 1975. The percentage of older Americans in poverty has stayed steady at roughly 10% since the mid-1990s. Although a smaller percentage of the elderly are in poverty than are people under 65, almost 3.6 million Americans aged 65 and older had family incomes below the federal poverty threshold in 2007.[14]

Although the poverty rate for all persons aged 65 and older was 9.7% in 2007, the poverty rates among women, minorities, single individuals, those with low education, and the oldest old were higher. (See **Figure 19**.) Twelve percent of women aged 65 and older were in poverty in 2007 compared with only 6.6% of men. Because women live longer, the number of poor older women in 2007 (2.5 million) was more than twice the number of poor older men (1.0 million). Poverty rates are especially high among minorities. In 2007, nearly one-quarter of elderly African- Americans and more than one-sixth of elderly Hispanics were in poverty. About 80% of all older Americans identify themselves as white. Thus, although only 7.4% of older white Americans were poor, poor whites comprised 60% of all poor elderly in 2007.

Older individuals with low education also had high poverty rates. Eighteen percent of those without a high school education had family incomes below the poverty line in 2007 compared with only 4.3% of those with a college degree. There is a significant difference in the poverty rates of married persons and single elderly individuals. Married couples, who often have more than one source of income, had a poverty rate of only 4.2% in 2007. In contrast, 16.2% of unmarried individuals aged 65 and older had incomes below the poverty threshold in 2007. The oldest Americans had the highest poverty rates. Among individuals 80 and older, 11.5% were poor in 2007, compared with 8.5% of those between the ages of 65 and 69.

## The Near-Poor

Many older Americans have family incomes that put them just above the official poverty threshold. In 2007, only 9.7% of people aged 65 and older had incomes below the poverty thresholds of $9,944 for an individual and $12,550 for a couple; however, another 13% of Americans aged 65 and older had family incomes between 100% and 149% of the poverty threshold. Also, whereas 11.5% of persons age 80 and older had incomes below the poverty threshold, another 17.4% of people age 80 and older had family incomes between 100% and 149% of the poverty threshold in 2007.

## CONCLUSION

Americans aged 65 and older receive income from a variety of sources. Although Social Security benefits, pensions, and income from assets are the most common income sources, earnings also are important, especially for those under age 70.

There are large disparities in the amounts and types of income that older Americans receive. Income from assets in the form of interest and dividends, for example, make up a significant percentage of the aggregate income of the elderly population. However, most elderly individuals receive only modest amounts of interest and dividend income, whereas a relatively small number of people receive large amounts of income from these sources. Social Security is both the largest source of aggregate income among the elderly and the biggest single source of income for a majority of Americans aged 65 and older. Compared to the great disparity in interest and dividend income, there is relatively little difference between the average monthly Social Security benefit and the highest monthly benefit. This is because the Social Security benefit formula limits the maximum amount paid to a retired high-wage earner to about 150% of the amount paid to a career-long average- wage worker.

Social Security and public assistance together provide more than 90% of all income for the poorest 25% of the elderly population. These public programs have contributed greatly to reducing poverty among the elderly. The reduction in poverty among older Americans is one of the most significant public policy successes of the past half-century. Poverty among those aged 65 and older has fallen from one in three older persons in 1960 to fewer than one in ten today. Although the overall rate of poverty is relatively low, it remains high for women, minorities, the less-educated, single persons, and those over age 80.

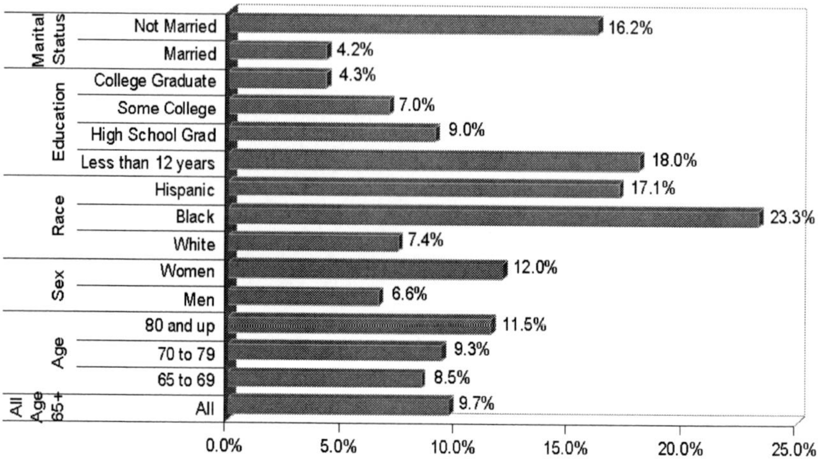


Source: CRS analysis of the March 2008 *Current Population Survey.*

Figure 19. Percentage of Individuals Aged 65 and Older in Poverty, 2007

# End Notes

1 This number does not include approximately 1.6 million elderly who live in nursing homes.

2 U.S. Census Bureau, *Income, Poverty, and Health Insurance Coverage in the United States, 2007*; P60-23 5, Table 3, p. 13, [http://www.census.gov/prod/2008pubs/p60-235 .pdf].

3 Family income differs from household income in households in which more than one family resides or in which a family resides with other unrelated individuals.

4 In Figure 10, the demographic traits are those of the individual who was designated as the householder on the CPS.

5 *Tax Reform Act of 1986*, P.L. 99-514. The *Pension Protection Act of 2006* (P.L. 109-280) further reduced the maximum vesting period in many plans to three years.

6 See CRS Report RL30496, *Pension Issues: Lump-Sum Distributions and Retirement Income Security*, by Patrick Purcell.

7 As reported here, "pension income" includes payments from a company or union pension, payments from a federal, state, or local government pension, military retirement pay, regular payments from an annuity or paid-up insurance policy, and regular payments from an IRA, Keogh account, or a §401(k)-type account. As defined on the CPS, pension income does not include lump-sum distributions from pension plans. To the extent that individuals receive lump-sum distributions from plans and later draw on those amounts to supplement their income, the CPS understates individual and household income from pension plans.

8 These numbers sum to 12.4 million. About 300,000 people had both types of pension.

9 U.S. Bureau of Labor Statistics, news release USDL 08-1344, *Employee Tenure in 2008*, September 26, 2008, at [http://www.bls.gov/news.release/tenure.nr0.htm].

10 Of 36.790 million individuals aged 65 and older in 2007, 35.485 million (96.5%) reported income from one or more sources and 18.889 million (51.3%) reported income from assets.

11 Of 25.483 million households with a householder or spouse aged 65 and older in 2007, 98.9% had income from any source and 4.476 million (56.8%) had income from assets.

[12] Joseph Quinn, "Retirement Trends and Patterns Among Older American Workers" in Stuart Altman and David Shactman (eds.), *Policies for an Aging Society* (Baltimore: Johns Hopkins University Press, 2002), pp. 293-315.

[13] For more information on the labor force participation of older workers, see CRS Report RL30629, *Older Workers: Employment and Retirement Trends*, by Patrick Purcell.

[14] The official poverty threshold in 2007 for a single person aged 65 or older was $9,944. The poverty threshold for a couple in which at least one member was 65 or older was $12,550. See *Poverty Thresholds 2007*, available at [http: //census. gov/ hhes/ www/ poverty/ threshld/ thresh07.html].

In: The Role of Savings and Other Issues… ISBN: 978-1-60741-446-9
Editor: Joel K. Harris 

*Chapter 4*

# CONVERTING RETIREMENT SAVINGS INTO INCOME: ANNUITIES AND PERIODIC WITHDRAWALS*

***Janemarie Mulvey and Patrick Purcell***

## SUMMARY

To a worker contemplating retirement, there is perhaps no more important question than "How long will my money last?" Congress has a strong interest in the income security of older Americans because much of their income is either provided directly from public programs like Social Security, or in the case of pensions and retirement accounts, is subsidized through tax deductions and deferrals.

Many retirees must decide how to convert retirement account balances into income and how to preserve the accounts in the face of several kinds of risk.

- *Longevity risk* is the risk that the individual will exhaust his or her account before death and experience a substantial decline in income.

---

* This is an edited, reformatted and augmented version of a CRS Report for Congress publication dated December 2008.

- *Investment risk* is the risk that the assets in which the individual has invested his or her retirement account will decline in value.
- *Inflation risk* is the risk that price increases will cause the individual's retirement income to decline in purchasing power.
- *Unexpected events* such as divorce, the death of a spouse, the cost of medical care, or a need for long-term care services are also risks.

There are strategies for dealing with each of these risks, but no single strategy can deal effectively with all of them. For example, purchasing a life annuity insures against longevity risk and it shifts the investment risk to the insurer. However, purchasing an annuity depletes the purchaser's available assets by the amount of the premium. These assets are no longer available to the retiree in the event of a catastrophic illness or other unexpected major expense. To date, the demand for annuities has been low. There are many reasons for the low demand for annuities, but one of the most important has been that many potential annuity purchasers do not value the longevity insurance provided by annuities at its market price.

Retirees who choose not to purchase life annuities must decide how much to withdraw from their retirement accounts each year. Because they face uncertainty with respect to both life expectancy and the rate of return on investment, this decision carries its own risks. If withdrawals are too large, retirees risk spending down their savings too quickly, possibly leaving them impoverished. If withdrawals are too small, they might spend too little and leave substantial assets unspent when they die.

An analysis conducted by CRS indicates that under specific conditions there is a 95% or greater probability that a man who retires at age 65 will not exhaust his retirement account before the earlier of death or age 95 if his initial withdrawal does not exceed 5% of the account balance and later withdrawals are the same in inflation-adjusted dollars. Under the same conditions, there is a 95% or greater probability that a woman who retires at age 65 will not exhaust her retirement account before the earlier of death or age 95 if her initial withdrawal does not exceed 4.5% of the account balance and later withdrawals are the same in inflation-adjusted dollars.

# INTRODUCTION

The 78 million members of the "baby boom" generation are beginning to retire.[1] After many years of accumulating assets to spend in retirement, they now must decide how to convert these assets into a steady stream of income. Because of the trend away from defined benefit (DB) pensions to defined contribution (DC) plans—such as 401(k) plans—future retirees will be less likely to have a guaranteed stream of income from defined benefit pensions. Furthermore, while Social Security will provide a guaranteed income to most retirees, it will replace only a relatively small proportion of their pre-retirement income.[2] As a result of these trends, many future retirees will rely greatly on their savings to finance their consumption during retirement.

A retiree who is deciding how to convert wealth into retirement income will have to balance many risks. Increases in average life expectancy will mean that future retirees will have to ensure that their wealth will last through a retirement that could span 30 or 40 years. Increased volatility in equity markets, the effects of inflation on purchasing power, and the possibility of substantial expenses for medical treatment and long-term care will further complicate this decision.

There are a number of ways to convert retirement wealth into income. One option is to purchase a life annuity from an insurance company. In exchange for payment of an initial premium, a life annuity pays a guaranteed income throughout retirement, regardless of how long the purchaser lives.[3] Life annuities represent only about 5% of individual annuities sold in the United States. Most annuities sold in the U.S. are deferred annuities, which are tax-deferred retirement savings accounts. At retirement, a deferred annuity can be converted to a life annuity; yet, relatively few deferred annuities are converted to life annuities. Likewise, most individuals who have accumulated retirement savings in 401(k) plans or individual retirement accounts (IRAs) choose to access these funds through lump-sum distributions or periodic withdrawals rather than by purchasing a life annuity.

There are many reasons why relatively few retirees choose to purchase a life annuity as a source of retirement income.[4] Among these reasons are that

- most retirees receive annuity income from Social Security;
- about one-third of retirees receive annuity income from defined benefit pensions;

- the fees charged by annuity providers can be high and the fee structure is not transparent;
- purchasing an annuity reduces the assets available to the retiree to meet unexpected expenses, and breaking the contract is costly; and
- there have been instances of deceptive sales practices by some agents, many of whom receive large commissions for each sale.

**Table 1. Estimated Percentage of Individuals Age 65 in 2004 Surviving to Selected Ages**

| Surviving to Age | Total | Male | Female |
|---|---|---|---|
| 75 | 66.6 | 60.3 | 72.7 |
| 80 | 53.9 | 46.5 | 61.0 |
| 85 | 38.3 | 30.6 | 45.4 |
| 90 | 22.2 | 15.9 | 27.8 |
| 95 | 9.4 | 5.8 | 12.4 |
| 100 | 2.5 | 1.3 | 3.5 |

Source: U.S. National Center for Health Statistics, National Vital Statistics Report, *United States Life Tables*, 2004, vol. 56(9), (December 2007).

Another option for converting retirement savings into income is to take periodic withdrawals from a retirement account. Some retirees attempt to "self-annuitize" by basing the amount of each periodic withdrawal from the account on their remaining life expectancies. Retirees who selfannuitize take on the responsibility of managing their investments and also the risk that they will live longer than average.

This chapter has two sections. The first section describes four kinds of risk that retirees face in retirement: longevity risk, investment risk, inflation risk, and the risk of large, unexpected expenses for medical care or long-term care. It then describes the basic features of life annuities and examines some of the reasons that the market for these annuities remains small, in spite of the protection that they provide against outliving one's retirement assets. The second section of the report describes various strategies for self-annuitizing and presents the results of an analysis that CRS conducted to estimate the probability that an individual who elects to self-annuitize would exhaust his or her retirement assets before death.

# The Nature of Risk in Retirement

Decisions about how to draw down assets in retirement must take into account many risks. These include longevity risk (i.e., the risk that one will live beyond the average life expectancy), inflation risk, investment risk, and the risk associated with unexpected financial shocks from widowhood, divorce, medical care, or the need for long-term care services.

## Longevity Risk

The U.S. population is living longer than previous generations. A man who reached age 65 in 1960 could expect to live another 13.0 years, while a woman who turned 65 in 1960 had a remaining life expectancy of 15.8 years. A man who reached age 65 in 2004 could expect to live another 17.1 years, while a woman who turned 65 in 2004 had a remaining life expectancy of 20.0 years.[5] Looking beyond the averages, more than one-fourth of women who reach age 65 are likely to live to age 90, and 12.4% are likely to live to age 95. One out of six men who attain age 65 will live to age 90, and an estimated 6% will live to age 95. (See **Table 1**). Individuals who underestimate the likelihood of living into very old age might spend their assets too quickly, depleting their savings while they still have many years to live. This could lead to a decline in their standard of living, and possibly to increased reliance on public assistance programs.

## Inflation Risk

As overall prices in the economy rise over time, the purchasing power of income declines unless income increases at the same rate that prices increase. Few pensions in the private sector provide regular cost-of-living increases. Data collected by the Department of Labor indicate that fewer than 5% of pensions in the private sector provide regular cost-of-living adjustments to retirees. Retirees must account for the potential impact of inflation on their investment portfolios as they decide how to draw down their retirement wealth.

Social Security is one of the few sources of retirement income that is fully inflation-indexed each year. Yet, even Social Security's annual cost-of-living adjustments may not fully protect retirement income from the effects of inflation. The annual cost-of-living adjustment for Social Security is based on the increase in the overall level of prices. Prices for some categories of expenditures that the elderly use at higher rates than younger consumers – such as health care – have been growing faster than overall prices. Over the period from 1980 to 2007, the average annual rate of inflation for goods and services averaged 3.5%, but prices for medical care rose at an average annual rate of 5.9%.[6] For those who have above-average out-of-pocket health care expenditures, these price increases can significantly reduce the amount of income available for other expenditures. In addition, Medicare Part B premium increases are tied to program cost increases which have historically exceeded growth in general inflation.[7] By 2025, these premiums are expected to equal over 50% of the average Social Security benefit, as compared to 27% in 2006.[8]

## Investment Ristk

Investment risk is the possibility that an individual's retirement assets might decline in value because specific stocks, bonds, or other assets depreciate. Diversification can reduce investment risk, because declines in the value of some assets are likely to be fully or partially offset by gains in the value of other assets. Stock and bond mutual funds, for example, help protect individuals from investment risk by purchasing securities from many companies in a variety of industries. In a mutual fund, investment losses from companies that are performing poorly may be offset by investment gains from companies that are performing well.

Investment risk includes market risk, which is the possibility that an individual's retirement assets will decline in value because of an overall decline in asset prices, as when the stock market falls. Even a well-diversified portfolio of stocks will not protect the value of an individual's retirement from depreciating if stock values fall across the board, as they have in 2008. Although a diversified portfolio can moderate investment risk, there have been extended periods of time when declines in the stock market and low interest rates resulted in negative returns on investment. For example, between 1929 to 2006 there were 14 ten-year periods of negative annual rates of return after adjusting for inflation. **Table 2** shows the five worst of those 14 ten- year periods. There have also been instances when negative rates of return spanned 15 years. Between 1966 and 1981, real rates of return on stocks averaged -

0.4%, and the average annual real rate of return on short-term government securities was -0.2%.[9] Those who retire at the beginning of a period of negative returns could face significant reductions in retirement wealth.

## Unexpected Events

Unexpected events can adversely affect retirement income. These include losing a spouse through death or divorce, high medical expenses, and the need for long-term care services. According to a recent study by the Urban Institute, more than two-thirds of adults age 70 and older experienced at least one such financial shock over a nine-year period. Widowhood occurred among nearly one-third of married adults over age 70. The study found that widowhood was more likely to reduce women's wealth than men's wealth.[10]

Unexpected health care costs can also reduce retirement wealth. Although the majority of retirees are covered by Medicare, deductibles and co-payments can be significant for those who are seriously ill. Medicare provides only limited coverage for long-term hospital stays and nursing home care. A recent analysis of the Health and Retirement Survey found that 6% of households aged 75-84 paid more than 50% of their income for out-of-pocket medical expenses.[11] These costs can be especially high at the end of life when a surviving spouse may face large medical bills and an accompanying reduction in retirement income. A study in 2002 found that out-of- pocket costs for end-of-life medical expenses could average about $23,000 (adjusted to 2007 dollars).[12] While the introduction of Medicare Part D may offset some of these costs, even under this program an individual who is not eligible for a low-income subsidy could be responsible for more than $6,000 in copayments for prescription medicines in 2009.

Another potential economic shock is the cost of long-term care services.[13] It has been estimated that over two-thirds of individuals aged 65 and older will require long-term care services at some point in their lives. In 2008, the annual average cost of a nursing home stay is $68,255 for a semiprivate room and $76,285 for a private room.[14] These costs greatly exceed the 2007 median income of $29,730 among households in which either the householder or householder's spouse was 65 or older.[15] Medicare does not cover extended stays in nursing homes, and Medicaid coverage generally is available only to individuals who are poor or become poor by spending down their assets on long-term care services.[16] For those who are not Medicaid-eligible and who have not purchased private long-term care insurance, long-term care costs must be paid out-of- pocket.

## ANNUITIES AS A SOURCE OF RETIREMENT INCOME

A life annuity – also called an immediate annuity – is an insurance contract that provides income payments on specified dates in return for an initial premium. Life annuities can help protect retirees against some of the financial risks of retirement, especially longevity risk and investment risk. Life annuities pay income to the purchaser for as long as he or she lives, and in the case of joint-and survivor annuities, for as long as the surviving spouse lives. In addition, some annuities offer limited protection against inflation through annual increases. However, the annual increases must be paid for by accepting a lower initial monthly annuity income. Other annuities allow the purchaser to share in the investment gains from growth in equity markets as a way to offset the effects of inflation; however, such annuities also require the purchaser to share in the investment losses if markets fall.

Despite the potential advantages of annuities in reducing longevity risk and investment risk, life annuities continue to represent a small proportion of all annuities sold in the U.S. In recent years, deferred annuities – used as tax-deferred savings vehicles – have outsold life annuities by a ratio of almost 20 to 1.[17] As noted earlier, the irrevocable nature of annuity contracts appears to be an important factor in dissuading many retirees from purchasing life annuities. Although insurers have devised options to assure that the payments will continue after the purchaser's death – jointand-survivor annuities, and term-certain annuities, for example – these options add to the cost of the annuity. Because of the projected increase in the number of older Americans over the next 20 years, and the concurrent increase in the potential market for life annuities, insurers are likely to continue to add features to their annuity products in an attempt to broaden their appeal to retirees.

### The Current Market for Annuities

Annuities are either provided through employer-sponsored pension plans (the group market) or are purchased directly by individuals (the individual market).

**Table 2. Annual Average Rate of Return over 10- Year Period (adjusted for inflation)**

| | Portfolio Mix | |
|---|---|---|
| **Time Period** | **65% Stocks/35% Bonds** | **65% Bonds/35% Stocks** |
| 1968 to 1978 | -4.3 | -1.8 |
| 1972 to 1982 | -4.0 | -1.7 |
| 1964 to 1974 | -3.9 | -1.3 |
| 1971 to 1981 | -3.8 | -1.6 |
| 1938 to 1948 | -3.6 | -3.4 |

Source: CRS analysis of data from Ibottson Associates.

### *Group Annuities*

Annuities from defined-benefit pensions can protect retirees from investment risk and longevity risk. The benefit formula under most defined benefit pensions is based on the worker's years of service and final average salary. The individual's benefit does not vary with investment returns, nor does it decrease as a result of increases in average life-expectancy.[18] The employer that sponsors the plan bears both the investment risk and the longevity risk. If investment returns fall below expectations, or if the plan's actuaries project increases in life expectancy, the plan sponsor must provide additional funding to the plan to meet these costs. Since the mid-1980s, the proportion of workers who retire with a defined benefit pension has declined substantially. The number of workers participating in defined benefit pension plans fell from 26.9 million in 1985 to 20.6 million in 2006, a decline of 23%.[19]

Another reason for the decline in the number of workers retiring with an employer-sponsored annuity has been an increase in the number of defined benefit plans that offer the option of taking a lump-sum rather than an annuity. Of all those who are covered under a defined benefit plan, more than half are offered the choice between a lump sum and an annuity.[20] When offered this choice, many individuals choose the lump-sum option. According to a study by the Vanguard Group, only 40% of defined benefit plan participants who are offered a lump-sum choose to receive an annuity.[21] Given these trends, the share of retirement income that will be guaranteed in the form of a defined benefit annuity is likely to decline in the future.

### *Individual Annuities*

Annuities purchased directly from insurance companies or from insurance agents or brokers by individuals are called individual annuities. Two features that vary across individual annuities are the timing of payments and the rates of return.

### Timing of Payments

Annuities can either be *deferred*, in that premiums are paid and assets are accumulated while the individual is working and payment of income is deferred until the worker retires, or *immediate*, in which a single premium is paid in exchange for lifelong stream of income that begins immediately.

A deferred annuity is similar to a savings account in which individuals can accumulate money over time. Investment earnings accrue on a tax-deferred basis. Deferred annuities represent nearly 95 percent of annuity sales. While individuals holding a deferred annuity can convert the funds into a guaranteed stream of income in retirement, most take a lump-sum payment or a series of periodic withdrawals.[22]

An immediate annuity provides a guaranteed monthly income for a specified period of time in exchange for a one-time premium payment. Income from an annuity can be either fixed or variable. Income from an annuity may be a received for specific number of years, as with a *term certain annuity*, for the life of the annuitant, as in a *single-life annuity*, or for the lives of both the annuitant and his or her spouse, as in a *joint and survivor annuity*. Under a joint and survivor annuity, the surviving spouse is eligible to receive income until he or she dies. The survivor benefit is typically 50%, 75%, or 100% of the income received while the annuity purchaser was living. As noted earlier, while immediate annuities can protect retirees from longevity risk and transfer the investment risk to the insurer, only 5% of individual annuities currently sold are immediate annuities.[23]

**Table 3** shows some examples of monthly income from an immediate annuity. Most annuities purchased in the private sector provide different incomes for men and women. Men can purchase an annuity with a higher monthly income than women for the same premium because the average life expectancy of a man is lower than for a woman of the same age. The average lifetime values of the annuities for a man and woman of the same age would be equal. Employer-sponsored pension plans must offer unisex annuities to retirees.[24] Under a unisex annuity, a man would receive a lower monthly annuity income than he would get from a gender-based annuity, reflecting the higher average life expectancy of a group that includes both men and women. Likewise a woman would receive a higher monthly annuity income from a unisex annuity than she would receive would from a gender-adjusted annuity.

**Rates of Return**

Annuities are similar to other investment vehicles in that purchasers earn a rate of return on their premium investment. The rate of return on the annuity can be fixed, indexed, variable, or some combination of the three. The risk, regulation and fee structure varies across these different types of annuities.

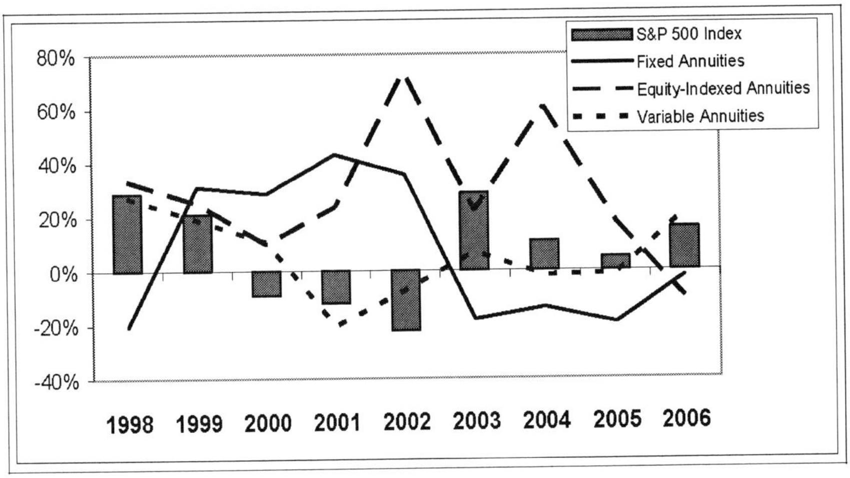


Source: CRS estimates based on data from National Association of Variable Annuity, 2007 Annuity Factbook. Data on growth in equity markets based on annual rate of return of S&P index reported by Ibbotson Associates.

Figure 1. Growth in Annuity Sales Relative to Growth in the S&P 500 Index

**Table 3. Monthly Income by Gender and Joint/Survivor Option for Fixed Annuity with a $100,000 Premium, 2008**

| | | Unisex | Male | Female |
|---|---|---|---|---|
| Age 60 | Single Life | 690 | 716 | 666 |
| | Joint and Survivor | 645 | 656 | 645 |
| Age 65 | Single Life | 714 | 801 | 734 |
| | Joint and Survivor | 657 | 721 | 707 |
| Age 70 | Single Life | 869 | 917 | 828 |
| | Joint and Survivor | 810 | 811 | 793 |

Source: Based on CRS Annuity Calculator. Assumes fixed real (inflation-adjusted) rate of return equal to historical average of 2.8%, and no added adjustments for adverse selection.

A *fixed annuity* pays a fixed monthly payment for the term of the annuity. The amount of the monthly payment is determined at the time the annuity is purchased. The income that any given premium amount will purchase depends mainly on the age of the purchaser (and the age of the purchaser's spouse in the case of a joint and survivor annuity) and prevailing market interest rates for medium-term bonds at the time the annuity is purchased. In 2007, fixed annuities represented 22% of annuity sales.[25]

A *variable annuity* offers annuity purchasers a choice of a wide range of investment options that can vary in value over time. The investment options can include stocks, bonds and money market portfolios. The monthly income provided by a variable annuity will fluctuate according to the investment performance of the funds in which the annuity premium is invested. Income from a variable annuity can decline if the investment underlying the annuity loses value. Some variable annuity policies offer limited protection against declines in value through a guaranteed minimum income. In 2007, the majority of annuity sales (67%) comprised variable annuities.[26]

An *equity-index* annuity earns a rate of return based on the performance of an equity index fund. Examples of equity indexes used include Dow Jones Industrial Average, Lehman Brothers Aggregate U.S. Index, and Standard and Poor's (S&P) 500 Composite Stock Price Index. If the underlying index declines, the income provided by the annuity will also decline. To reduce this risk, the insurer in some cases may provide a guaranteed minimum payment to protect the consumer against market fluctuations. This minimum, however, costs more to annuity purchasers by reducing their initial annuity income. In 2007, 11% of annuity sales were indexed annuities.[27]

The demand for each type of annuity is influenced by rates of return in equity markets. A strong equity market reduces demand for fixed annuities while a weak stock market increases demand for fixed annuities. During the strong equity market in late 1990s, growth in variable annuities sales exceeded growth in fixed annuity sales. By early 2000, when equity markets were earning negative rates of return, the demand for variable annuities fell. After 2000, growth in variable annuity sales dominated the market. (See **Figure 1**.)

## Inflation Protection Options

Inflation-indexed annuities preserve the purchasing power of annuity income by providing a lifetime stream of income that increases with inflation. Treasury Inflation Protected Securities (TIPS) could be used as an investment vehicle by insurers that would like to offer inflation- indexed annuities, but few U.S. insurers offer such annuities. Potential purchasers have proven unwilling to accept a substantially lower initial payment in exchange for protection against inflation. Some insurers offer *graded annuities* that provide annual increases in payments, which are typically capped at 3%, but graded annuities do not fully protect against inflation that exceeds the annual cap.

## Tax Treatment of Annuities

The taxation of an annuity differs between the accumulation phase and the payout phase. Deferred annuities receive favorable tax treatment in the accumulation phase. Returns on investment are not taxed in the year they are earned. During the payout phase, taxation of annuity income differs between payments taken as withdrawals and payments taken as a life annuity. In either case, annuity income is taxed at ordinary income tax rates rather than at capital gains tax rates.[28] The taxation of annuity income depends on whether the income is received as

- a single lump sum,
- a series of withdrawals that are not annuitized, or
- a life annuity (either variable or fixed).

When funds are withdrawn as a lump sum, the amount of the distribution that exceeds the amount the annuity owner invested is subject to taxation at the owner's ordinary income tax rate.[29] If money is taken out of the annuity in a series of withdrawals, each withdrawal is considered to consist of investment earnings until all investment gains have been withdrawn.[30] The taxation of annuity income is summarized in Table 4.

### *Taxation of Income from a Fixed Annuity*

Each payment from a fixed annuity is treated as consisting partly of the investment gains, which are taxable, and partly as a return of principal, which is not taxable. The proportion of each payment that is excluded from taxable income is determined by dividing the amount that the individual paid into the annuity by the total amount that would be paid out over an average life expectancy, according to life tables published by the Internal Revenue Service. Each payment is multiplied by this ratio to determine the fraction of the annuity payment that is not subject to income taxes. For example, consider an individual who has paid a $100,000 premium for an immediate annuity at age

65. In November 2008, a 65 year-old male would receive monthly income of about $675 for a premium of $100,000. IRS life tables indicate that, on average, the purchaser will receive annuity payments for 20 years.[31] The total expected lifetime income from the annuity therefore would be $162,000.[32] The proportion of each payment that would be excluded from taxable income would be 100,000/162,000, or 61.7%. The other 38.3% percent of each payment would be subject to income taxes.

### *Taxation of Income from a Variable Annuity*

With a variable annuity, income varies with the performance of the underlying investments. The amount of income from a variable annuity that is excluded from taxable income is computed by dividing the premiums paid for the annuity by the number of years that payments are expected to be made to the annuitant. For a life annuity, this would be the annuitant's life expectancy as determined using IRS tables. In the case of a 65 year-old who had paid a premium of $100,000, the amount of each monthly annuity payment that would be excluded from taxable income would be $416.[33]

### *Tax Exclusion for Long-Term Care Insurance*

An exception to the taxation of annuity income was included in the Pension Protection Act of 2006 (P.L. 109-280). Beginning in 2010, withdrawals from annuity contracts that are used to pay for qualified long-term care insurance premiums are not subject to income tax. However, the investment in the annuity contract is reduced by the amount of the long-term care insurance premiums. This means that a larger percentage of the future income received from the annuity will represent investment gains and will be subject to income taxes.

## Consumer Protections and the Regulatory Environment

Consumer protections are intended to ensure that information used to sell an annuity is truthful, and that individuals who purchase an annuity fully understand the future consequences with respect to retirement income. The key challenge in the development and enforcement of consumer protections is that some annuity products are regulated exclusively at the state level while others are also regulated by federal agencies. Because state governments have primary jurisdiction over regulation of fixed annuities, there is wide variation in regulation across states. Further, while variable annuities are regulated by the federal Securities and Exchange Commission (SEC), equity-index annuities, which are designed to track the performance of a common stock index, such as the S&P 500 or the Russell 2000, are regulated primarily by the states.

**Table 4. Tax Treatment of Annuities**

| Type of Account | Individual's Contributions | Investment Returns | Withdrawals |
|---|---|---|---|
| Deferred Annuity | After-tax | Tax-Deferred | Amounts in excess of contributions are taxed as ordinary income |
| Immediate Annuity | After-tax | Not applicable | Amounts in excess of contrib as ordinary income |
| Defined Benefit Pension | Varies[a] | Tax-deferred | Amounts not previously included in taxable income ta income |

Source: Congressional Research Service.

a. In the private-sector, employee contributions are rarely required. Federal employee pension contributions are made with after-tax income. Tax treatment of pension contribution by state and local employees varies by locality.

### *State Regulation of Annuities*

Like other insurance products, most annuities are regulated by the states. State laws govern the organization and licensing of insurance companies and their agents and state insurance departments oversee insurance company operations. These state laws and regulations also govern marketing and sales practices as well as insurer requirements.

To help guide states in their oversight efforts, the National Association of Insurance Commissioners (NAIC) has developed language for "model laws and regulations" to provide guidelines for legislators to modify and adopt in their respective states. The NAIC Model Act has not been uniformly adopted across states, thus leaving potential gaps in consumer protections. As of February 2008, 17 states have not adopted the NAIC model regulations on suitability.[34] The NAIC Model Suitability language requires insurance companies to give objective financial information to potential purchasers, and it requires agents to use a standardized form to determine whether an annuity would be suitable for the potential purchaser. Some state laws ban the use of professional designations or titles – such as Senior Financial Advisor – that might mislead senior consumers into thinking the advisor has special financial expertise related to the needs of older consumers.

A similar problem exists with respect to disclosure requirements in annuity contracts. The NAIC Annuity Disclosure Model Regulation requires certain information to be disclosed, including information about premiums and how they are charged, a summary of the options and restrictions for accessing money, and an outline of fees. According to the NAIC, 35 states have adopted the NAIC disclosure regulation.

The states also play a role in protecting annuity owners against the insolvency of annuity insurers. To do this, each state has a state guaranty association to provide a financial safety net for each line of insurance and to ensure that coverage continues if an insurer becomes insolvent. State laws require insurers to become members of the guaranty associations in every state in which they are licensed to do business. The actual coverage for annuity contracts varies from state to state, but cash values and annuity benefits are usually protected up to at least $100,000. However, coverage is not provided for variable annuity contracts. Variable annuity contracts are held in separate accounts by insurers and they are protected from the general creditors of the insurance company in the event of insolvency. Although the Securities Investor Protection Corporation (SIPC) protects against fraud in variable annuity sales, it does not provide any relief to investors whose variable annuities decline due to falling prices in equity markets.

### *Federal Regulation of Annuities*

Because the assets underlying variable annuities are invested in equities, they are regulated by the federal government through the Securities and Exchange Commission (SEC). Equity-index annuities, which are based on market indexes, are not yet regulated by the SEC (see discussion below). Federal securities laws require certain disclosure documents, including a prospectus, to be given to investors. Certain disclosure documents must also be filed with the SEC. In addition, written marketing materials, such as advertisements, are subject to federal regulation.

Federal law prohibits agents who sell variable annuities from making untrue statements of material fact or failing to state a material fact that is necessary to prevent the statement from being misleading.[35] Annuity agents also have a fiduciary duty to provide full and fair disclosure of all material facts to their clients and their prospective clients, including all statements in advertising materials. Currently, equity-index annuities are regulated by the states, rather then the SEC. To address this inconsistency in regulation between variable and equity-index annuities, the Securities and Exchange Commission has issued a proposed regulation that would extend federal securities laws with respect to full and fair disclosure and sales practice protections to certain equity-index annuities.[36]

## Why Is Demand for Individual Annuities So Low?

Despite some of the potential advantages of individual life annuities, immediate annuities remain a small part of retirement assets held in the U.S. Of those who purchased immediate annuities in 2003, the median age of purchase was 70.[37] The Internal Revenue Code requires owners of individual retirement accounts to begin taking withdrawals from their accounts and including the withdrawals in their taxable income no later than April of the year in which they reach age 70½.. Some owners of IRAs use immediate annuities to meet the requirement to take these "required minimum distributions" from their retirement accounts. Without this requirement, demand for annuities might even be lower.

There are several reasons why the demand for annuities is low despite the aging of the population. Some potential purchasers may already feel they have a sufficient amount of annuitized income from Social Security, and about a third of people 65 and older also have annuity income from defined benefit pensions. Another reason may be the amount and non- transparency of fees and expenses charged by insurance companies. Further, annuity contracts are not easily canceled, and many individuals fear that after purchasing an annuity they may later need a large sum of money to pay for unexpected expenses, such as long-term care or health expenses. Even among people who understand that it is important to insure against longevity risk, some fear that they will die before reaching their normal life expectancy, and will end up "losing the bet" with the insurance company that sold the annuity. Finally, recent adverse publicity about deceptive sales practices in the annuity market has added to concerns among potential buyers of immediate annuities.

### *Complexity and Lack of Transparency in Annuity Expenses*

Annuity providers impose a number of fees and expenses that are complex and are not transparent to the annuity purchaser. Even a rather "simple" prospectus identifying the various fees can be more than 50 pages long.[38]

Fees and expenses fall into three main categories: surrender charges, investment fees, and insurance charges. Fees and expenses vary depending on the type of annuity (fixed or variable). Both fixed and variable annuities have surrender charges, which are fees for cancelling the contract before a specified number of years have passed. A typical surrender charge starts at 7% of the premium in the first year of the contract and declines by 1% a year until it reaches zero. However, a few companies have surrender charges of up to 15% to 25% of the annuity premium.[39]

Variable annuities have two additional fees associated with managing assets. These are investment management fees and insurance charges. Investment management fees cover the cost of managing the different funds across investment accounts. Investment fees vary depending on the type of investment portfolio chosen. Insurance charges include administration, sales commissions, and mortality and expense charges. Mortality and expense charges average 1.15% of the average value of investment and cover three components of the insurance guarantee:

- Mortality premium or guarantee of income over one's lifetime;
- Death benefit to protect beneficiaries (also called survivor benefit); and,
- The cost of the minimum income guarantee.

These fees vary by product design. Typically, a fixed annuity with a joint and survivor option is subject to all three components. However, a variable annuity without a joint and survivor option and no minimum guarantee would only be subject to the mortality premium.

It is difficult for consumers to identify and understand each fee charged for an annuity. Each insurer has a different format for disclosing information. The insurance industry has recognized this problem and has begun to standardize fee disclosure. A group of insurance organizations is working to develop a simple, standardized disclosure document that presents information about fees in a consumer-friendly manner.[40]

Another factor affecting the cost of annuities is that people who buy annuities tend to be those who expect to live longer than average. A person who chooses to purchase an annuity may have information about his or her health, habits, or family history that the insurance company does not have regarding their risk of living longer than average. This phenomenon, called "adverse selection," leads to higher annuity premiums than insurers would otherwise have to charge if longevity risk were spread over the entire population. Estimates of the cost of adverse selection vary. Some studies have found that adverse selection reduces income to annuity purchasers by 4 cents to 10 cents per dollar of premiums paid.[41] A more recent study defined “potential annuitants” more narrowly to only include those with sufficient wealth to purchase an annuity. When re-defined in this manner, potential annuitants tend to live considerably longer than average and thus would receive a better deal from an annuity than the average person. According to this analysis, the impact of adverse selection on annuity prices is only about half as great as previously estimated, or about 2 cents to 5 cents per premium dollar.[42] If participation in individual annuities were broader, the effect of adverse selection would be reduced and annuitants’ income would be higher.

***Lack of Flexibility in Dealing with Unexpected Expenses***

Once an individual purchases an immediate annuity, the decision is not easily reversible. Most states require a 10-day look back period during which a buyer can change his or her mind, but after this, canceling an annuity contract will result in substantial surrender charges. Part of the lack of flexibility in annuity contracts was recently addressed in the Pension Protection Act of 2006, which allows funds used to purchase an annuity to be withdrawn tax-free to buy long-term care insurance. It is important to note that long-term care insurance must be purchased well in advance of actually needing long-term care services. Annuity owners would have to make the decision to purchase long-term care insurance in the early years of the payout phase.

Dying Before Getting Full Value. Annuity buyers pay for the insurance component of the annuity, which guarantees a monthly income no matter how long the annuitant lives. Some people are reluctant to purchase an annuity out of fear that they will die before they get back the premiums that they paid into it. Joint and survivor annuities and term-certain annuities can assure that annuity payments will continue even if the purchaser dies earlier than he or she expected, but these options reduce the monthly payments that the annuitant receives while he or she is living.

Adverse Publicity and Lack of Knowledge About Annuities. Another factor affecting current demand for annuities may be adverse publicity surrounding false advertising and deceptive sales practices employed by insurance agents selling equity-index annuities. These practices may have led some consumers to avoid all annuity products. Equity-index annuities, however, currently account for only 11% of annuity sales. Further, recent proposals by the SEC to strengthen regulations for sales of equity-index annuities may help to alleviate consumers’ concerns in the future.

## RETIREMENT ACCOUNT WITHDRAWAL STRATEGIES

Although annuities offer protection from longevity risk and investment risk, relatively few people use their retirement savings to purchase an annuity. Most people choose instead to take periodic withdrawals from their retirement accounts. Individuals who purchase life annuities transfer the responsibility for managing assets and the risk of outliving their assets to an insurance company. In contrast, retirees who "self-annuitize" take on the responsibility of managing their investments and also the risk of living longer than average. Annuity purchasers, however, give up control over the assets that they use to purchase their annuities, while those who take periodic withdrawals have the money in their retirement accounts available to meet large, unexpected expenses that may arise during retirement.

For those who choose to take periodic withdrawals, there are two basic approaches to taking money out of their retirement accounts. The first approach attempts to "smooth" consumption over the period of retirement through equal (inflation-adjusted) withdrawals each year. This method provides a steady income from year to year, but as the examples presented in this chapter will illustrate, it can be difficult to choose a rate of withdrawal that can be sustained in the face of uncertain life expectancy and variable rates of return on investment. Another strategy for drawing down retirement assets is to take withdrawals that are based on the individual's remaining life expectancy in the year that each withdrawal is taken. This method of withdrawing money from a retirement account is prescribed by law for the *required minimum distributions* that all owners of traditional IRAs and retired owners of 401(k) accounts must begin taking after they reach age 70½.[43] Under this approach, it is unlikely that the individual will exhaust his or her savings, but withdrawals can vary substantially from year to year. This can make planning and budgeting difficult.

An individual who chooses to take periodic withdrawals might want to have some idea how likely his or her chosen strategy is to succeed. The first step in such an assessment is to define success. Financial planners often advise clients that they should adopt a method of withdrawing retirement funds that will result in a high probability that their savings will last 30 to 40 years. Assuming that 40 years is a reasonable upper bound for the number of years that a retirement account might need to last, the next task for the retiree is to determine the minimum probability of success that he or she is willing to accept. There is no fixed standard for the minimum probability of success that a retiree should be willing to accept for the annual rate of withdrawal that he or she chooses. For purposes of illustration, we have highlighted in the tables that follow the combinations of initial withdrawal rates and investment allocations that resulted in an account balance lasting for a given number of years (or to a given age) in 95.0% or more of our simulations.

## How Long Will a Retirement Account Last with Fixed Annual Withdrawals?

One way to evaluate the likely success of a withdrawal strategy is to determine the probability that the retiree's assets will last for at least a specific number of years, assuming that rates of return on investment will vary from year to year. To estimate this probability, CRS developed a model that estimates how long a sum of money will last, assuming a particular initial rate of withdrawal and the probable distribution of annual rates of return on investment. The model estimates the annual rate of return on investment through a Monte Carlo simulation process in which the rate of return in each year is based on the distribution of annual total returns on stocks and bonds over the 82 years from 1926 through 2007.[44] (See **Appendix A** for a description of Monte Carlo simulation processes.)

It is important to note that an annual rate of withdrawal that minimizes the risk of exhausting a retirement account – whether by delaying the initial withdrawal or by taking "small" annual withdrawals – will increase the likelihood that the account will have substantial assets remaining at the time of the owner's death. Delaying the initial withdrawal and taking relatively small withdrawals both help to preserve assets in the event that the individual outlives his or her normal life expectancy or experiences below-average rates of investment return. However, for the individual who lives to his or her normal life expectancy and experiences average rates of return on investment, the end result of successfully reducing the risk of exhausting his or her account may be a substantial unexpended account balance at the time of death.

### Initial Rate of Withdrawal

CRS estimated the probability that assets would last for five periods of time ranging from 20 years to 40 years at five initial withdrawal rates ranging from 4.0% to 6.0% of the value of the account when the first withdrawal is taken. We chose this range of withdrawal rates because "a large body of research on 'safe' withdrawal rates for individuals has determined that a real withdrawal rate in the neighborhood of 4 percent of the initial retirement portfolio has a 'low' chance of running out of money,"[45] and because recent research has demonstrated that initial rates of withdrawal equal to 7.0% or more are very likely to exhaust the assets too rapidly.[46] In the estimates presented in the following tables, the withdrawal rate is stated as the percentage of the *initial* withdrawal from the account. Subsequent withdrawals are equal to the first withdrawal in constant (inflation-adjusted) dollars, but they may represent a different percentage of the remaining account balance.[47]

## Investment Portfolio

Many financial advisors recommend that retirees should keep 50% or more of their retirement savings invested in a diversified portfolio of stocks because stocks have historically achieved a higher long-run average rate of return than bonds. The higher long-run average rate of return on common stocks compared to bonds acts as a form of longevity insurance for the retiree. Generally, advisors recommend that the remainder of assets should be invested in bonds and money market securities that are less susceptible than stocks to large capital losses.

In our analysis, we simulated withdrawals from two portfolios. In one set of simulations, retirees allocated 65% of assets to the *Standard & Poor's 500* index of stocks and invested the remainder in AAA-rated corporate bonds. In the second set of simulations, retirees allocated 35% of assets to the *Standard & Poor's 500* index of stocks and invested the remainder in AAA-rated corporate bonds. In all of the simulations, withdrawals were taken at the beginning of each year. Accounts were re-balanced annually so that the portfolio would start each year at the chosen allocation between stocks and bonds. The model also took into account the correlation between annual returns on stocks and bonds.[48] The effects of account fees and income taxes were ignored for purposes of this analysis.[49]

### *Probability of Assets Lasting for at Least a Specific Number of Years*

The data presented in **Table 5** illustrate the likelihood that savings will last for at least a given number of years under several initial rates of withdrawal and under the two investment portfolios described above. Panel 1 of **Table 5** shows the probability that a retirement account will last for at least a given number of years, assuming that 65% of the assets in the account are invested in stocks represented by the *Standard & Poor's 500* index and 35% of the assets are invested in AAA-rated corporate bonds. Panel 2 of Table 5 shows the probability that savings will last for at least a given length of time, assuming that 35% of the assets are invested in stocks and 65% of the assets are invested in bonds.[50]

**Table 5. Estimated Probability a Retirement Account Will Last for at Least a Specific Number of Years**

| Probability that Money Will Last: | Initial Annual Withdrawal from Retirement Account | | | | |
|---|---|---|---|---|---|
| | **4.0%** | **4.5%** | **5.0%** | **5.5%** | **6.0%** |
| **Panel 1: Investment Portfolio = 65% Stocks, 35% Bonds** | | | | | |
| 20 years or more | *98.5* | *96.9* | 94.1 | 89.8 | 84.2 |
| 25 years or more | *95.7* | *92.3* | 87.0 | 80.7 | 72.3 |
| 30 years or more | 92.5 | 87.2 | 80.5 | 72.6 | 63.3 |
| 35 years or more | 89.6 | 82.7 | 75.3 | 66.4 | 56.3 |
| 40 years or more | 86.8 | 78.3 | 71.0 | 61.7 | 51.4 |
| **Panel 2: Investment Portfolio = 35% Stocks, 65% Bonds** | | | | | |
| **Probability that money will last:** | | | | | |
| 20 years or more | *99.7* | *98.9* | 96.4 | 92.2 | 84.8 |
| 25 years or more | *97.7* | *94.5* | 87.8 | 78.3 | 65.2 |
| 30 years or more | 94.0 | 87.3 | 77.0 | 64.1 | 49.5 |
| 35 years or more | 89.4 | 79.7 | 66.9 | 53.2 | 38.8 |
| 40 years or more | 84.3 | 73.2 | 58.9 | 45.6 | 31.1 |

Source: Congressional Research Service.

Notes: Probabilities >= 95.0% are in italics.

### *Portfolio of 65% Stocks and 35% Bonds*

The results presented in **Table 5** indicate that at an initial withdrawal rate of 4.0%, there is a 98.5% probability that an account invested in this portfolio will last for at least 20 years. The longer the period of time over which withdrawals are taken, the lower the likelihood that a given rate of withdrawal will continue to be successful. At a 4.0% initial rate of withdrawal, there is a 92.5% chance that the account will last for 30 years or more, and an 86.8% chance that it will last for at least 40 years.

For any given number of years, the likelihood of an account lasting for at least that length of time is lower for higher initial rates of withdrawal. While there is a 98.5% chance that an account will last for at least 20 years at a 4.0% initial rate of withdrawal, this probability drops to 94.1% for a 5.0% initial rate of withdrawal and to 84.2% for a 6.0% initial rate of withdrawal.

***Portfolio of 35% Stocks and 65% Bonds***

Panel 2 of **Table 5** shows the probability that a retirement account in which 35% of assets are invested in stocks and 65% of assets are invested in bonds would last for at least 20, 30, or 40 years. The results of the simulations indicate that for periods of time of 20 years or more, the likelihood of exhausting a retirement account is higher for an account with a 65% allocation to bonds compared to an account with a 65% allocation to stocks.

The likelihood that an account would last for at least 20 years is slightly higher for an account with a 65% allocation to bonds compared to an account with a 65% allocation to stocks. This result occurs because a portfolio that is more heavily invested in stocks has a greater chance than a portfolio mainly invested in bonds of experiencing a large capital loss. If this happens in the early years of retirement, the account may be depleted rapidly. Over longer periods of time, however, the probability of running out of money is substantially higher with a portfolio in which 65% of assets are invested in bonds compared to a portfolio in which 65% of assets are invested in stocks because of the lower expected average annual rate of return on bonds.

## Estimates Incorporating Life Expectancy

The estimates presented in **Table 5** illustrate the probability that a retirement account will last for at least a given number of years, assuming a particular initial rate of withdrawal, a specific allocation of investments between stocks and bonds, and the estimated annual rates of return on investment. These results are likely to underestimate the likelihood that a particular strategy will succeed because they do not account for individual mortality. Because not all account owners will live until the end of a fixed interval of time, the probability of an account having money in it at the *earlier* of either the account owner's death or the end of the interval is greater than the probability of the account having money in it at the end of the interval. To ignore the possibility of the account owner dying in any year will result in underestimating the probability that a particular rate of withdrawal will sustain the account throughout the owner's lifetime. As other researchers have noted, the relevant consideration in planning retirement withdrawals is "the probability of running out of money in the retirement life span, whether that span is shorter or longer than a predetermined number of years."[51]

Estimates of the likelihood that a retirement account will last for a particular number of years should include the probability that the account owner will survive for that number of years. This can be done by including in the model of retirement withdrawals the probability of the individual surviving from one year to the next. To incorporate the effect of mortality on the probability that a retiree will exhaust his or her retirement account before the earlier of either the retiree's death or the attainment of a particular age, CRS added two variables to its model. One variable accounts for the individual's age at retirement and in each succeeding year, and the other makes each annual withdrawal conditional on the individual having survived from one year to the next.[52] The probability of survival from year to year was based on male and female life expectancies taken from cohort life tables.[53] An individual's withdrawal strategy was considered to have been successful if there was a 95.0% or higher probability that he or she had a positive account balance in the year of death or, if still living, at the ages of 80, 85, 90, 95, and 100.

**Table 6, Table 7,** and **Table 8** show the estimated probabilities that the retirement accounts of men and women who retire at ages 60, 65, or 70 will last until the ages of 80, 85, 90, 95, and 100, taking into account the probability of the individual dying in each year.[54] The initial withdrawal rates range from 4.0% to 6.0% and subsequent withdrawals are assumed to be equal in real value (i.e., adjusted for inflation) to the initial withdrawal.[55] The tables show the estimated probabilities of success for two portfolios. In one portfolio, 65% of assets are invested in stocks and 35% in bonds, and in the other portfolio, 65% of assets are invested in bonds and 35% in stocks.

The data presented in **Table 6** show the estimated probabilities of a retirement account lasting until ages 80, 85, 90, 95, and 100 for men and women retiring at age 60. **Table 5** showed that at a 4.0% initial rate of withdrawal from an account invested 65% in stocks and 35% in bonds, there is a 98.5% chance that a retirement account will last for at least 20 years. The results presented in **Table 6** show that under the same set of assumptions, but incorporating the effects of mortality, a man retiring at 60 has a 99.1% chance that his retirement account will last until at least age 80, while for a woman retiring at age 60 there is a 98.9% chance that her account will last until at least age 80. In this case, the probabilities are almost equally high in both **Table 5** and **Table 6**, and there is little difference in the probabilities of success between and women. Both of these results change for the probability of success at later ages.

**Table 5** showed that at a 4.0% withdrawal rate, the probability of a retirement account lasting for at least 30 years was 92.5%. The data in **Table 6** show that once the effects of mortality are taken into consideration, there is a 97.3% chance that a man who retires at 60 and takes an initial withdrawal of 4.0%, will still have some money in the account at age 90, while a woman retiring at age 60 and taking an initial withdrawal of 4.0% has a 96.1% chance of still having money in her account on her 90$^{th}$ birthday. The probability that a woman will still have money in her account at any given age is lower than the probability for a man because a woman has a higher probability of having survived to that age. (See **Appendix B.**)

In simulations representing retirement at age 60, a withdrawal rate of 4.0% was successful in 95.0% or more of simulations for both men and women under both investment portfolios at all ages up to 100. (See **Table 6**.) A withdrawal rate of 6.0% failed to achieve a 95.0% success rate for either men or women under either investment portfolio even just to age 80. For both men and women retiring at age 60, a withdrawal rate of 5.0% or higher carries a high risk that their retirement accounts will be exhausted before they have attained their normal life expectancies.

**Table 7** and **Table 8** show that, compared to retiring at age 60, delaying retirement until 65 or 70 can substantially increase the likelihood that an individual will not exhaust his or her retirement account before he or she dies. In simulations representing retirement at age 65, withdrawal rates of 4.0% and 4.5% were successful in 95.0% or more of simulations for both men and women under both investment portfolios at all ages up to 100. (See **Table 7**.) A withdrawal rate of 6.0% achieved a 95.0% success rate under either investment portfolio for both men and women only up to age 80. For men who retire at age 65, a withdrawal rate of 5.5% or higher carries a substantial risk that their retirement accounts will be exhausted if they live to age 90 or older. For women who retire at age 65, a withdrawal rate of 5.0% or higher carries a substantial risk that their retirement accounts will be exhausted if they live to age 90 or older.

In simulations representing retirement at age 70, withdrawal rates of 4.0%, 4.5%, and 5.0% were successful in 95.0% or more of simulations for both men and women under both investment portfolios at all ages up to 100. (See **Table 8**.) A withdrawal rate of 5.5% was successful up to age 100 in 94.7% or more of cases for men under either investment portfolio, but succeeded in 95.0% or more of cases only to age 90 for women. For men who retire at age 70, a withdrawal rate of 6.0% or higher carries a substantial risk that their retirement accounts will be exhausted if they live to age 95 or older. For women who retire at age 70, a withdrawal rate of 5.5% or higher carries a substantial risk that their retirement accounts will be exhausted if they live to age 95 or older.

**Table 6. Probability of Retirement Account Lasting to at Least a Given Age, Including Mortality Risk, Retirement at Age 60**

| Probability that Money Will Last at Least Until: | Initial Annual Withdrawal from Retirement Account | | | | |
|---|---|---|---|---|---|
| | **4.0%** | **4.5%** | **5.0%** | **5.5%** | **6.0%** |
| **Panel 1: Male Retiring at Age 60, Portfolio = 65% Stocks, 35% Bonds** | | | | | |
| Age 80 | *99.1* | *98.1* | *96.4* | 93.5 | 89.8 |
| Age 85 | *98.1* | *96.3* | 93.2 | 89.6 | 84.8 |
| Age 90 | *97.3* | *95.0* | 91.4 | 87.3 | 82.6 |
| Age 95 | *97.0* | 94.4 | 90.6 | 86.4 | 81.9 |
| Age 100 | *96.9* | 94.3 | 90.5 | 86.3 | 81.7 |
| **Panel 2: Male Retiring at Age 60, Portfolio = 35% Stocks, 65% Bonds** | | | | | |
| Age 80 | *99.8* | *99.4* | *98.1* | 95.1 | 90.8 |
| Age 85 | *99.1* | *97.6* | 94.1 | 89.1 | 82.5 |
| Age 90 | *98.1* | *95.8* | 91.4 | 85.6 | 78.6 |
| Age 95 | *97.7* | *95.0* | 90.4 | 84.3 | 77.1 |
| Age 100 | *97.5* | 94.8 | 90.1 | 84.1 | 76.9 |
| **Panel 3: Female Retiring at Age 60, Portfolio = 65% Stocks, 35% Bonds** | | | | | |
| Age 80 | *98.9* | *97.8* | *95.5* | 92.7 | 88.3 |
| Age 85 | *97.5* | *95.6* | 91.6 | 87.0 | 81.7 |
| Age 90 | *96.1* | 93.6 | 89.0 | 83.7 | 78.3 |
| Age 95 | *95.5* | 92.8 | 87.7 | 82.5 | 77.0 |
| Age 100 | *95.3* | 92.6 | 87.4 | 82.2 | 76.6 |
| **Panel 4: Female Retiring at Age 60, Portfolio = 35% Stocks, 65% Bonds** | | | | | |
| Age 80 | *99.7* | *99.2* | *97.5* | 94.4 | 88.6 |
| Age 85 | *98.4* | *96.7* | 92.8 | 86.9 | 77.7 |
| Age 90 | *96.9* | 94.3 | 88.2 | 81.2 | 71.7 |
| Age 95 | *96.1* | 92.8 | 86.1 | 78.9 | 69.4 |
| Age 100 | *95.7* | 92.3 | 85.4 | 78.4 | 69.0 |

Source: Congressional Research Service.

Notes: Probabilities >= 95.0% are in italics.

**Table 7. Probability of Retirement Account Lasting to at Least a Given Age, Including Mortality Risk, Retirement at Age 65**

| Probability that Money Will Last at Least Until: | Initial Annual Withdrawal from Retirement Account | | | | |
|---|---|---|---|---|---|
| | 4.0% | 4.5% | 5.0% | 5.5% | 6.0% |
| **Panel 1: Male Retiring at Age 65, Portfolio = 65% Stocks, 35% Bonds** | | | | | |
| Age 80 | *99.9* | *99.7* | *99.3* | *98.6* | *96.9* |
| Age 85 | *99.3* | *98.4* | *97.3* | *95.1* | 91.9 |
| Age 90 | *98.7* | *97.0* | *95.5* | 92.6 | 88.5 |
| Age 95 | *98.3* | *96.4* | 94.8 | 91.6 | 87.3 |
| Age 100 | *98.1* | *96.2* | 94.6 | 91.4 | 87.1 |
| **Panel 2: Male Retiring at Age 65, Portfolio = 35% Stocks, 65% Bonds** | | | | | |
| Age 80 | *>99.9* | *>99.9* | *>99.9* | *99.6* | *98.7* |
| Age 85 | *99.8* | *99.5* | *98.5* | *96.6* | 92.5 |
| Age 90 | *99.3* | *98.2* | *96.2* | 92.8 | 87.3 |
| Age 95 | *98.9* | *97.4* | *95.0* | 91.3 | 85.5 |
| Age 100 | *98.7* | *97.1* | 94.6 | 90.9 | 85.1 |
| **Panel 3: Female Retiring at Age 65, Portfolio = 65% Stocks, 35% Bonds** | | | | | |
| Age 80 | *99.9* | *99.7* | *99.1* | *98.2* | *97.0* |
| Age 85 | *99.0* | *98.1* | *96.3* | 93.8 | 90.9 |
| Age 90 | *97.8* | *96.3* | 93.5 | 89.7 | 86.0 |
| Age 95 | *97.1* | *95.5* | 92.2 | 87.8 | 83.9 |
| Age 100 | *96.9* | *95.1* | 91.8 | 87.4 | 83.4 |
| **Panel 4: Female Retiring at Age 65, Portfolio = 35% Stocks, 65% Bonds** | | | | | |
| Age 80 | *>99.9* | *>99.9* | *99.9* | *99.5* | *98.3* |
| Age 85 | *99.9* | *99.2* | *98.1* | *95.5* | 90.9 |
| Age 90 | *99.1* | *97.3* | 94.3 | 90.1 | 82.9 |
| Age 95 | *98.3* | *95.7* | 92.1 | 87.3 | 79.6 |
| Age 100 | *98.0* | *95.2* | 91.2 | 86.4 | 78.8 |

Source: Congressional Research Service.

Notes: Probabilities >= 95.0% are in italics.

**Table 8. Probability of Retirement Account Lasting to at Least a Given Age, Including Mortality Risk, Retirement at Age 70**

| Probability that Money Will Last at Least Until Age: | Initial Annual Withdrawal from Retirement Account | | | | |
|---|---|---|---|---|---|
| | 4.0% | 4.5% | 5.0% | 5.5% | 6.0% |
| **Panel 1: Male Retiring at Age 70, Portfolio = 65% Stocks, 35% Bonds** | | | | | |
| Age 80 | *>99.9* | *>99.9* | *>99.9* | *99.9* | *99.9* |
| Age 85 | *>99.9* | *99.8* | *99.4* | *98.5* | *97.9* |
| Age 90 | *99.7* | *99.0* | *98.1* | *96.2* | 94.5 |
| Age 95 | *99.4* | *98.4* | *97.4* | *95.0* | 92.9 |
| Age 100 | *99.3* | *98.1* | *97.1* | 94.7 | 92.6 |
| **Panel 2: Male Retiring at Age 70, Portfolio = 35% Stocks, 65% Bonds** | | | | | |
| Age 80 | *>99.9* | *>99.9* | *>99.9* | *>99.9* | *>99.9* |
| Age 85 | *>99.9* | *>99.9* | *99.9* | *99.6* | *99.0* |
| Age 90 | *99.9* | *99.7* | *98.9* | *97.6* | *95.2* |
| Age 95 | *99.6* | *99.1* | *97.7* | *95.6* | 92.4 |
| Age 100 | *99.5* | *98.8* | *97.2* | *95.1* | 91.7 |
| **Panel 3: Female Retiring at Age 70, Portfolio = 65% Stocks, 35% Bonds** | | | | | |
| Age 80 | *>99.9* | *>99.9* | *>99.9* | *>99.9* | *99.9* |
| Age 85 | *99.9* | *99.7* | *99.4* | *98.6* | *97.7* |
| Age 90 | *99.5* | *98.6* | *97.4* | *95.2* | 93.1 |
| Age 95 | *98.8* | *97.6* | *95.9* | 93.3 | 90.6 |
| Age 100 | *98.5* | *97.2* | *95.3* | 92.6 | 89.9 |
| **Panel 4: Female Retiring at Age 70, Portfolio = 35% Stocks, 65% Bond** | | | | | |
| Age 80 | *>99.9* | *>99.9* | *>99.9* | *>99.9* | *>99.9* |
| Age 85 | *>99.9* | *99.9* | *99.9* | *99.6* | *99.0* |
| Age 90 | *99.9* | *99.4* | *98.5* | *96.5* | 93.2 |
| Age 95 | *99.4* | *98.4* | *96.6* | 93.4 | 88.7 |
| Age 100 | *99.1* | *97.9* | *95.7* | 92.3 | 87.6 |

Source: Congressional Research Service.

Notes: Probabilities >= 95.0% are in italics.

## Estimates of Variable Annual Withdrawals

The estimates shown in **Table 5, Table 6, Table 7,** and **Table 8** are based on simulations of a withdrawal strategy that produces annual income of a constant real (inflation-adjusted) amount. The individual takes an initial annual withdrawal equal to a particular percentage of the account balance, and all subsequent withdrawals are equal to the real value of the initial withdrawal. In this respect, the withdrawal strategy mimics an inflation-indexed annuity by providing a steady annual income.[56] However, an individual who self-annuitizes must, in effect, insure against his or her own longevity by holding substantial "reserves" in the account to protect against the possibility of outliving his or her savings. Because insurers diversify the risk of longevity over all annuity purchasers, they are able to pay a higher annual income than an individual who selfannuitizes could safely withdraw from his or her account. Taking withdrawals from a retirement account that are equal to the amount that would be paid by an annuity purchased from an insurance company exposes the retiree to the risk of outliving his assets.[57]

If a retiree is willing to allow the amount withdrawn from the account to vary from year to year based on investment returns and remaining life expectancy, he or she can reduce the likelihood of fully depleting the account before dying. The trade-off for reducing this risk is that the individual's annual income will be less predictable. This can make planning and budgeting more difficult. One such strategy bases each annual withdrawal on the current account balance and the individual's remaining life expectancy.[58] This withdrawal rule is mandated under the Internal Revenue Code for owners of traditional IRAs and retired owners of 401(k) plans after they attain age 701/2 "to ensure that retirees consume their tax-qualified retirement pension accounts instead of leaving them as bequests for their heirs."[59]

**Table 9, Table 10,** and **Table 11** show how annual withdrawals that are based on the individual's remaining life expectancy in the year that the withdrawal is taken can vary over the course of the person's retirement. **Table 9** illustrates the variability of withdrawals for a man and a woman each of whom retires at age 60 with an account balance of $100,000. **Table 10** and **Table 11** show withdrawals for men and women who retire at ages 65 and 70, respectively, also with initial account balances of $100,000.[60] In 2004, a 60 year-old man had a remaining life expectancy of 20.8 years and a woman had a remaining life expectancy of 24.0 years.[61] Under the $1/E(t)$ withdrawal rule, the 60 year-old man would withdraw 1/20.8 (4.8%) of his account balance and the 60 year-old woman would withdraw 1/24.0 (4.2%) of her account. One year later, the 61 year- old man would have a remaining life expectancy of 20.0 years and would withdraw 1/20.0 (5.0%) of his account balance. The 61 year-old woman would have a remaining life expectancy of 23.2 years and would withdraw 1/23.2 (4.3%) of her account balance. As the retiree ages, his or her remaining life expectancy falls, and the percentage of the account that he or she withdraws rises. At age 75, for example, a man has a remaining life expectancy of 10.7 years and so he would withdraw 1/10.7 (9.3%) of his remaining account balance. A 75 year-old woman has a remaining life expectancy of 12.8 years and would withdraw 1/12.8 (7.8%) of her remaining account balance.

Under this method, annual withdrawals are a continually rising fraction of the remaining account balance, but the real dollar of value of the withdrawals may rise or fall from year to year, depending on the investment performance of the retirement account. In a "worst-case scenario" the aging retiree's withdrawals would be a rising fraction of a shrinking account balance. Although the retiree would not fully deplete the account—because the withdrawal is never equal to 100% of the remaining account balance—if the account shrinks in value due to a decline in asset values, the withdrawals could grow smaller from year to year.[62]

Withdrawals based on remaining life expectancy will vary in size (measured here in constant dollars) from year to year. For example, the top panel of **Table 9** shows the range of withdrawals taken between the ages of 60 and 100 by a man who retires at age 60 with an account balance of $100,000. Across 10,000 simulations, the typical male retiree could expect his annual withdrawals to range from $4,465 to $9,160 with an average withdrawal of $6,394. In 5% of the simulations, however, the *smallest* annual withdrawal was $1,409 or less, and in 5% of the simulations, the *largest* withdrawal was $22,803 or more. A woman with the same portfolio retiring at age 60 could expect her annual withdrawals to range from $3,940 to $9,729 with an average withdrawal of $6,342. (See Panel 3 of **Table 9**. In 5% of the simulations, the smallest annual withdrawal was $1,530 or less, and in 5% of the simulations, the largest withdrawal was $25,968 or more.

Panels 2 and 4 of **Table 9** show that when the simulations were based on a portfolio in which 65% of assets were invested in bonds and 35% invested in stocks, the average withdrawal was smaller than in the case of the more stock-heavy portfolio. The typical male retiring at 60 with a $100,000 portfolio invested 65% in bonds and 35% in stocks could expect his annual withdrawals to range from $4,491 to $7,370 with an average withdrawal of $5,734. (Again, all amounts are in constant dollars.) In 5% of all the simulations, however, the smallest annual withdrawal was $1,100 or less, and in 5% of the simulations, the largest withdrawal was $13,184 or more. A woman with the same portfolio who retires at age 60 could expect her annual withdrawals to range from $3,985 to $7,465, with an average withdrawal of $5,516. (See Panel 4 of **Table 9**.) In 5% of all the simulations, the smallest annual withdrawal was $1,349 or less, and in 5% of the simulations, the largest withdrawal was $14,460 or more.

For individuals who retire at age 65 or at age 70, average annual withdrawals will be higher than for those who retire at 60 because they will be based on shorter remaining life expectancies. **Tablc 10** shows the estimated range of withdrawals taken between the ages of 65 and 100 by men and women who retire at age 65 with initial account balances of $100,000. **Table 11** shows the estimated range of withdrawals taken between the ages of 70 and 100 by men and women who retire at age 70 with initial account balances of $100,000.[63]

For a man retiring at age 65 with an initial account balance of $100,000 of which 65% is invested in stocks and 35% is invested in bonds, annual withdrawals could be expected to range from $5,284 to $9,103 with an average withdrawal of $6,861. (See Panel 1 of **Table 10**.) In 5% of the simulations, however, the smallest annual withdrawal was $1,460 or less and in 5% of the simulations the largest withdrawal was $19,513 or more. A woman with the same portfolio retiring at age 65 could expect her annual withdrawals to range from $4,653 to $9,293 with an average withdrawal of $6,582. In 5% of the simulations, the smallest annual withdrawal was $1,554 or less, and in 5% of the simulations, the largest withdrawal was $22,126 or more.

For a man retiring at age 70 with an initial account balance of $100,000 of which 65% is invested in stocks and 35% is invested in bonds, annual withdrawals could be expected to range from $6,241 to $9,552 with an average withdrawal of $7,606. (See Panel 1 of **Table 11**.) In 5% of the simulations, however, the smallest annual withdrawal was $1,412 or less, and in 5% of the simulations, the largest withdrawal was $17,822 or more. A woman with the same portfolio retiring at age 70, could expect her annual withdrawals to range from $5,504 to $9,282 with an average withdrawal of $7,083. In 5% of the simulations, the smallest annual withdrawal was $1,519 or less, and in 5% of the simulations, the largest withdrawal was $19,314 or more.

## SUMMARY OF WITHDRAWAL STRATEGIES: BALANCING RISKS

The uncertainties that retirees face with respect to both life expectancy and annual rates of return on investment make choosing a withdrawal strategy for their retirement accounts one of the most complicated financial decisions of their lives. The decision is even more complicated if retirement assets must be managed over the joint life expectancies of a couple. In light of these complex considerations, some analysts have suggested that "the withdrawal phase of retirement planning may well require more professional guidance and expertise than the accumulation phase."[64]

**Table 9. Variable Annual Withdrawals Based on Life Expectancy, Retirement at Age 60 (account balance at age 60 = $100,000)**

| | Annual Withdrawal Based on Remaining Life Expectancy | | |
|---|---|---|---|
| | 5th Percentile | Median | 95th Percentile |
| **Panel 1: Male Retiring at Age 60, Portfolio = 65% Stocks, 35% Bonds** | | | |
| Smallest withdrawal | 1,409 | **4,465** | 4,818 |
| Mean withdrawal | 3,857 | **6,394** | 12,781 |
| Largest withdrawal | 4,818 | **9,160** | 22,803 |
| **Panel 2: Male Retiring at Age 60, Portfolio = 35% Stocks, 65% Bonds** | | | |
| Smallest withdrawal | 1,100 | **4,491** | 4,818 |
| Mean withdrawal | 3,978 | **5,734** | 8,845 |
| Largest withdrawal | 4,818 | **7,370** | 13,184 |
| **Panel 3: Female Retiring at Age 60, Portfolio = 65% Stocks, 35% Bonds** | | | |
| Smallest withdrawal | 1,530 | **3,940** | 4,168 |
| Mean withdrawal | 3,589 | **6,342** | 13,638 |
| Largest withdrawal | 4,378 | **9,729** | 25,968 |
| **Panel 4: Female Retiring at Age 60, Portfolio = 35% Stocks, 65% Bonds** | | | |
| Smallest withdrawal | 1,349 | **3,985** | 4,168 |
| Mean withdrawal | 3,729 | **5,516** | 9,061 |
| Largest withdrawal | 4,311 | **7,465** | 14,460 |

Source: Congressional Research Service.

**Table 10. Variable Annual Withdrawals Based on Life Expectancy, Retirement at Age 65 (account balance at age 65 = $100,000)**

| | Annual Withdrawal Based on Remaining Life Expectancy | | |
|---|---|---|---|
| | 5th Percentile | Median | 95th Percentile |
| **Panel 1: Male Retiring at Age 65, Portfolio = 65% Stocks, 35% Bonds** | | | |
| Smallest withdrawal | 1,460 | **5,284** | 5,851 |
| Mean withdrawal | 4,331 | **6,861** | 12,146 |
| Largest withdrawal | 5,851 | **9,103** | 19,513 |
| **Panel 2: Male Retiring at Age 65, Portfolio = 35% Stocks, 65% Bonds** | | | |
| Smallest withdrawal | 1,146 | **5,210** | 5,851 |
| Mean withdrawal | 4,442 | **6,270** | 9,025 |
| Largest withdrawal | 5,851 | **7,689** | 12,572 |
| **Panel 3: Female retiring at Age 65, portfolio = 65% Stocks, 35% Bonds** | | | |
| Smallest withdrawal | 1,554 | **4,653** | 5,006 |
| Mean withdrawal | 4,044 | **6,582** | 12,761 |
| Largest withdrawal | 5,006 | **9,293** | 22,126 |
| **Panel 4: Female Retiring at Age 65, Portfolio = 35% Stocks, 65% Bonds** | | | |
| Smallest withdrawal | 1,233 | **4,648** | 5,006 |
| Mean withdrawal | 4,097 | **5,901** | 9,059 |
| Largest withdrawal | 5,006 | **7,541** | 13,303 |

Source: Congressional Research Service.

**Table 11. Variable Annual Withdrawals Based on Life Expectancy, Retirement at Age 70 (account balance at Age 70 = $100,000)**

| | Annual Withdrawal Based on Remaining Life Expectancy | | |
|---|---|---|---|
| | 5th Percentile | Median | 95th Percentile |
| **Panel 1: Male Retiring at Age 70, Portfolio = 65% Stocks, 35% Bonds** | | | |
| Smallest withdrawal | 1,412 | **6,241** | 7,285 |
| Mean withdrawal | 4,935 | **7,606** | 12,127 |
| Largest withdrawal | 7,285 | **9,552** | 17,822 |
| **Panel 2: Male Retiring at Age 70, Portfolio = 35% Stocks, 65% Bonds** | | | |
| Smallest withdrawal | 1,230 | **6,172** | 7,285 |
| Mean withdrawal | 5,029 | **7,285** | 9,694 |
| Largest withdrawal | 7,285 | **8,511** | 12,512 |

| | Annual Withdrawal Based on Remaining Life Expectancy | | |
|---|---|---|---|
| | 5th Percentile | Median | 95th Percentile |
| **Panel 3: Female Retiring at Age 70, Portfolio = 65% Stocks, 35% Bonds** | | | |
| Smallest withdrawal | 1,519 | **5,504** | 6,164 |
| Mean withdrawal | 4,584 | **7,083** | 12,239 |
| Largest withdrawal | 6,164 | **9,282** | 19,314 |
| **Panel 4: Female Retiring at Age 70, Portfolio = 35% Stocks, 65% Bonds** | | | |
| Smallest withdrawal | 1,273 | **5,479** | 6,164 |
| Mean withdrawal | 4,661 | **6,552** | 9,365 |
| Largest withdrawal | 6,164 | **7,978** | 12,741 |

Source: Congressional Research Service.

A retiree who wishes to achieve a predictable annual income can take annual withdrawals that are equal in inflation-adjusted dollars. An individual who chooses a rate of withdrawal that is too high risks spending down the account too quickly, possibly leaving the person impoverished. An individual who chooses a rate of withdrawal that is too low risks spending down the account too slowly, unnecessarily reducing his or her consumption and leaving substantial assets unspent at death. On the other hand, the retiree can choose to take withdrawals that vary from year to year based on the current balance in the account and the retiree's remaining life expectancy. This strategy can result in highly variable annual income.

The results of the analysis that CRS conducted indicate that under certain conditions there is a 95.0% or greater probability a man who retires at age 65 will not fully deplete his retirement account before the earlier of his death or age 90 if his initial withdrawal does not exceed 5.0% of the account balance and if later withdrawals are equal to the first in inflation-adjusted dollars. Under the same conditions, there is a 95.0% or greater probability that a woman who retires at age 65 will not fully deplete her retirement account before the earlier of her death or age 90 if her initial withdrawal does not exceed 4.5% of the account balance and if later withdrawals are equal to the first in inflation-adjusted dollars. The results hold for both a portfolio invested 65% in stocks and 35% in bonds and for one invested 35% in stocks and 65% in bonds.

The weight that individuals assign to each of the risks they face in retirement will vary from person to person. No one withdrawal strategy will be optimal for everyone. Other researchers have noted that "overall ... there is no clearly dominant strategy, because all involve trade-offs between risk, benefit, and bequest measures, and individual preferences may vary."[65] One way to balance these risks would be to segregate one's retirement funds into two or more accounts and adopt different withdrawal strategies for each. Likewise, one might use some retirement assets to purchase an annuity while taking withdrawals from one or more accounts using one or more withdrawal strategies. Many retirees, however, will not have accumulated enough retirement savings to make these options practical.

# APPENDIX A. WHAT IS "MONTE CARLO" ANALYSIS?

*Monte Carlo* analysis is a method of estimating the probable outcome of an event in which one or more of the variables affecting the outcome are random. The term was coined by mathematicians in the 1940s who likened probability analysis to studying the games of chance played in the casinos of Monte Carlo. One common use of Monte Carlo simulations is to illustrate how the variability of investment rates of return can affect the balances in a retirement account. The essence of a Monte Carlo estimation process is to simulate an event many times, allowing the random variable to vary according to its mathematical mean and variance. Each outcome is then ranked according to the likelihood of its occurrence. Using Monte Carlo methods, analysts can estimate not just the result that will occur "on average," but also the likelihood of results that are significantly above or below the average. In other words, Monte Carlo methods of estimation allow us to incorporate into our estimates the element of *risk*.

Monte Carlo estimation methods utilize not just the average value of a random variable, but also the distribution of values around the average. For example, rates of return in the stock market vary from year to year. The nominal rate of return on the *Standard & Poor 's 500* index of stocks averaged 10.3% between 1926 and 2007, but annual rates of return varied widely around this average, producing a standard deviation of 20.0%. Likewise, while the nominal annual return on AAA-rated corporate bonds averaged 6.3% between 1926 and 2007, the standard deviation around this average was 7.0%.

To estimate the likely rate of return that an investment would achieve over a 40-year period, for example, Monte Carlo simulation software generates a rate of return for each year based on the distribution of probable rates of return, as derived from historical data. The program then simulates the 40-year period a second time, again generating a rate of return for each year from the probability distribution of rates of return. The process is repeated until the simulation is completed, and thousands of 40-year investment periods have been simulated. The results of the simulation—in this case, investment rates of return—are then ranked by percentiles. The model CRS used also accounted for the correlation between the rates of return on stocks and bonds and the effects of inflation on real annual returns.

In our simulation of a 40-year period in which 100% percent of assets were invested in common stocks, the mean real rate of return in 10,000 iterations (simulating a 40-year period 10,000 times) was 7.0%, which is the same as the actual mean real rate of return on common stocks in the period from 1926 through 2007. (1.103/1.0305 = 1.70) However, in 5% of those 10,000 iterations, the mean real rate of return over the 40-year period was 1.6% or less, while at the other extreme, in 5% of the 10,000 iterations, the mean real rate of return over the 40-year period was 12.4% or more. In terms of evaluating risk, these results imply an expected annual average real rate of return on common stocks over any given 40-year period of 7.0%, and a 90% probability that the average annual real rate of return over that period will be between 1.6% and 12.4%.

# APPENDIX B. UNITED STATES LIFE TABLES, 2004

**Table B-1. Life Expectancy at Each Age, in Years**

| Age | Men | Women |
|---|---|---|
| 60 | 20.8 | 24.0 |
| 61 | 20.0 | 23.2 |
| 62 | 19.3 | 22.4 |
| 63 | 18.5 | 21.6 |
| 64 | 17.8 | 20.8 |
| 65 | 17.1 | 20.0 |
| 66 | 16.4 | 19.2 |
| 67 | 15.7 | 18.4 |
| 68 | 15.0 | 17.7 |
| 69 | 14.4 | 16.9 |
| 70 | 13.7 | 16.2 |
| 71 | 13.1 | 15.5 |

| Table B-1 (Continued) | | |
|---|---|---|
| 72 | 12.5 | 14.8 |
| 73 | 11.9 | 14.1 |
| 74 | 11.3 | 13.5 |
| 75 | 10.7 | 12.8 |
| 76 | 10.2 | 12.2 |
| 77 | 9.6 | 11.5 |
| 78 | 9.1 | 10.9 |
| 79 | 8.6 | 10.3 |
| 80 | 8.2 | 9.8 |
| 81 | 7.7 | 9.2 |
| 82 | 7.3 | 8.7 |
| 83 | 6.9 | 8.2 |
| 84 | 6.5 | 7.7 |
| 85 | 6.1 | 7.2 |
| 86 | 5.7 | 6.8 |
| 87 | 5.4 | 6.3 |
| 88 | 5.0 | 5.9 |
| 89 | 4.7 | 5.6 |
| 90 | 4.4 | 5.2 |
| **Age** | **Men** | **Women** |
| 91 | 4.2 | 4.9 |
| 92 | 3.9 | 4.5 |
| 93 | 3.7 | 4.2 |
| 94 | 3.4 | 3.9 |
| 95 | 3.2 | 3.7 |
| 96 | 3.0 | 3.4 |
| 97 | 2.8 | 3.2 |
| 98 | 2.6 | 3.0 |
| 99 | 2.5 | 2.8 |
| 100+ | 2.3 | 2.6 |

Source: U.S. Department of Health and Human Services, National Center for Health Statistics, *National Vital Statistics Reports*, vol. 56, no. 9, December 28, 2007, Tables 2 and 3.

## End Notes

[1] The Bureau of the Census defines the baby boom as people born between 1946 and 1964.

[2] The Social Security Administration estimates that Social Security replaces about 55% of earnings for a career-long low-wage worker, 41% of earnings for a career-long median-wage worker, and 27% of earnings for a career-long high- wage worker.

[3] Life annuities are also sometimes called immediate annuities. This chapter uses these terms interchangeably.

[4] Some individuals choose not to spend assets because they wish to leave the assets as a bequest to their heirs. However, given that an individual chooses to spend some or all of his or her retirement savings, the relevant question for this analysis is why relatively few choose to do so by purchasing a life annuity.

[5] U.S. National Center for Health Statistics, National Vital Statistics Report, *United States Life Tables, 2004*, Vol. 56(9), (Dec. 2007).

[6] From 1980 to 2007, the Consumer Price Index (CPI) for all goods and services rose from 82.4 to 207.3 while the CPI for medical care rose from 74.9 to 351.1. See Council of Economic Advisers, *Economic Report of the President, February 2008,* Table B-60, p. 295.

[7] See CRS Report RL33364, *The Impact of Medicare Premiums on Social Security Beneficiaries*, by Kathleen Romig,.

[8] CRS estimates based on data reported in CMS Office of the Actuary Memorandum, "Additional Information Regarding Comparisons of Beneficiary Income and Out-of-Pocket Costs For Medicare Supplementary Medical Insurance." March 25, 2008.

[9] Siegel, Jeremy J. *Stocks for the Long-Run*. 2nd ed. New York: McGraw-Hill. 1998.

[10] Johnson, R., et al. "When the Nest Egg Cracks: Financial Consequences of Health Problems, Marital Status Changes, and Job Layoffs at Older Ages," *Urban Institute*, 2006.

[11] Jonathan Skinner, "Are You Sure You're Saving Enough for Retirement?" *Journal of Economic Perspectives*, 21(3), (Summer 2007), p. 59-80.

[12] Hoover, D., S. Crystal, R. Kumar, U. Sambamoorthi, and J. Cantor, "Medical Expenditures During the Last Year of Life: Findings from the 1992-1996 Medicare Current Beneficiary Survey," *Health Services Research*, 37(6), p. 1625- 1642, 2002.

[13] Long-term care refers to a broad range of medical, personal, and supportive services needed by individuals who can no longer care for themselves due to physical or cognitive impairments.

[14] Genworth Financial 2008 Cost of Care Survey, April 2008.

[15] This median income is based on the 99% of households with any income. See CRS Report RL32697, *Income and Poverty Among Older Americans in 2007*, by Patrick Purcell.

[16] The Medicaid statute prohibits individuals from transferring their assets to others in order to qualify for Medicaid. The law also protects some of the income and assets of the community spouse of a nursing home resident so that he or she is not impoverished.

[17] National Association of Variable Annuities, 2007 Factbook.

[18] Although annuity payouts vary depending on the age of retirement, these payouts are not tied to an individual's own life expectancy but rather that of a group of individuals.

[19] Pension Benefit Guaranty Corporation, *Pension Insurance Data Book, 2006.*

[20] Bureau of Labor Statistics, *2007 National Compensation Survey.*

[21] G. Mottola, and S. Utkus, "Lump Sum or Annuity? An Analysis of Choice in DB Pension Payouts," Vanguard Center for Retirement Research, vol. 30, November 2007.

[22] *National Association of Variable Annuities, 2007 Factbook.*

[23] *National Association of Variable Annuities, 2007 Factbook.*

[24] The United States Supreme Court ruled in 1983 that under federal civil rights statutes, employer-sponsored retirement plans cannot offer annuities that differentiate on the basis of gender. See *Arizona Governing Comm. v. Norris*, 463 U.S. 1073 (1983).

[25] *National Association of Variable Annuities, 2007 Factbook.*

[26] Ibid.

[27] *National Association of Variable Annuities, 2007 Factbook.*

[28] The long-term capital gains tax rate, as enacted in the 2003 Jobs and Growth Tax Relief Reconciliation Act, is 15%. Annuity withdrawals are taxed at the marginal tax rate for ordinary income, which could be higher than the capital gains tax rates.

[29] Annuities purchased in the individual market are purchased with after-tax income. The amount of any distribution from an annuity that represents a return to the purchaser of his or her own premium payments is not taxed a second time.

[30] For example, if someone invested $25,000 in a deferred annuity and the value of the annuity when he or she begins to take withdrawals is $50,000, the first $25,000 withdrawn is taxable as ordinary income. The remaining $25,000 is not taxed because it is considered a return of principal to the purchaser.

[31] See IRS Publication 939, *General Rule for Pensions and Annuities*, Table 5, p 25.

[32] 675 x 12 x 20 = 162,000.

[33] In the IRS tables, the individual's life expectancy at 65 is 20 years, or 240 months. 100,000/240 = 416.

[34] *American Council of Life Insurers*, "Life Insurers' Initiative to Improve the Annuity Sales Environment," Factsheet, February 2008.

[35] Section 17(a) of the Securities Act of 1934, Section 10(b) of the Exchange Act and Rule 10b-5, and Section 206 of the Investment Advisors Act of 1940

[36] See CRS Report RS22974, *Annuities and the Securities and Exchange Commission Proposed Rule 151A*, by Baird Webel.

[37] M. Drinkwater, "Annuitization Study: Profiles and Attitudes," LIMRA International, 2003.

[38] *Best's Review*, "Tis a Gift to be Simple: Complex Annuities Scare Off Both Buyers and Advisers, So the Industry is Offering Less Intimidating Products," April 1, 2006.

[39] Testimony of Minnesota Attorney General Lori Swanson Before the Senate Special Committee on Aging on "Advising Seniors About Their Money: Who is Qualified and Who is Not?" September 5, 2007.

[40] Members of this group include American Council of Life Insurers, National Association of Variable Annuities, National Association of Insurance and Financial Advisors, and the National Association of Independent Life Brokerage Agents.

[41] Mitchell, Olivia, James Poterba, Mark Warshawsky, and Jeffrey Brown, "New Evidence on the Money's Worth of Individual Annuities." *American Economic Review*, 89(5), 1999.

[42] Webb, Anthony. "Is Adverse Selection in the Annuity Market A Big Problem?" Issue Brief, Center for Retirement Research at Boston College, January 2006, Number 40.

[43] See 26 U.S.C. §401(a)(9) and §408(a)(6) and CRS Report RL31770, *Individual Retirement Accounts and 40[1](k) Plans: Early Withdrawals and Required Distributions*, by Patrick Purcell.

[44] We used the real annual rates of total return on the Standard and Poor's 500 index of common stocks (and its predecessor S& P index) and AAA-rated corporate bonds from 1926 through 2007 to represent the rates of return on investment. The Monte Carlo simulations were performed with Palisade Corporation's @RISK simulation software.

[45] J.J. Spitzer, J.C. Strieter, and S. Singh, "Guidelines for Withdrawal Rates and Portfolio Safety During Retirement," *Journal of Financial Planning*, vol. 20(10), (October 2007).

[46] Spitzer, Strieter, and Singh note that simulations of withdrawal rates of 7.0% or more of the account balance "invariably resulted in unnacceptable runout rates."

[47] This is mathematically equivalent to increasing an initial nominal withdrawal by the estimated annual rate of change in the consumer price index. As Spitzer, et al. (2007) note: "Some authors used nominal rates of return and then adjusted the withdrawals each year for inflation such that the withdrawal amount was the same amount in real terms. We chose to use real dollars throughout and avoid the annual inflation adjustment. The outcomes of either process should be the same irrespective of where the adjustment for inflation is made, whether in the withdrawal rate or in the rate of return earned by the investment."

[48] Over the period from 1926 through 2007, the correlation coefficient for the real rates of return on the S&P 500 index and AAA-rated long-term corporate bonds was .236.

[49] In reviewing the literature on retirement account withdrawals, we found that research studies were about evenly divided between those that simulated the effects of fees and taxes and those that did not. Since the purpose of our analysis was to illustrate the effects of rates of

withdrawal, rates of return on investment, and life expectancy on account balances, we decided to focus on these variables and ignore fees and taxes.

50 For these simulations, the initial account balance was assumed to be $100,000; however, the results are independent of the initial balance and apply equally to other amounts.

51 R.G. Stout and J.B. Mitchell, "Dynamic Retirement Withdrawal Planning, *Financial Services Review*, vol. 15(2), (Summer 2006). The authors further note that, "by incorporating the uncertain retirement life span, [a model of phased withdrawals] generates a more meaningful probability of financial ruin." Stout and Mitchell's analysis looked at one portfolio consisting of 65% stocks and 35% bonds, and their estimates were based on a unisex life expectancy table. CRS tested two portfolios, one of 65% stocks and one of 35% stocks, and we used separate life expectancy tables for men and women.

52 In each simulation, the individual's probability of having died between age x and age x+1 was compared to a random number generated by the model. If the random number was greater than the probability of having died, the simulation continued for another year. If the random number was lower than the probability of death, the simulation stopped.

53 Male and female life expectancies at each age were taken from "United States Life Tables, 2004," *National Vital Statistics Reports*, vol. 56(9), U.S. Department of Health and Human Services, Centers for Disease Control and Prevention, National Center for Health Statistics, (December 2007), available at http://www.cdc.gov/nchs/data/nvsr/ nvsr56/nvsr56_09.pdf.

54 Relatively few people take withdrawals from retirement accounts before age 60 because withdrawals from a traditional IRA or a 401(k) plan taken before age 591/2 are subject to a 10% additional tax except for certain situations defined in law at 26 U.S.C. §72(t). Section 401(a)(9) of the Internal Revenue Code requires owners of traditional IRAs and retired owners of 401(k) plans to start taking distributions after they reach age 70½.

55 As with the estimates shown in Table 5, for the results presented in Table 6, Table 7, and Table 8, the initial account balance was assumed to be $100,000, but the results are independent of the initial balance and would also apply to other initial account balances.

56 Most annuities are not adjusted for inflation, and the income therefore declines in value over time.

57 Ivica Dus, Raimond Maurer, and Olivia Mitchell, "Betting on Death and Capital Markets in Retirement: A Shortfall Risk Analysis of Life Annuities Versus Phased Withdrawal Plans," *Financial Services Review*, vol. 14(3), (Fall 2005).

58 In this method of withdrawing funds, the fraction withdrawn from the account each year is equal to 1/E(t), where E(t) is the person's remaining years of life expectancy at each age.

59 Dus, Maurer, and Mitchell, *Financial Services Review*, (2005).

60 The initial account balance is assumed to be $100,000 only for illustrative purposes. With a smaller initial balance, withdrawals would be smaller, but the relative variability of the withdrawals from year to year would be similar. Data from the Census Bureau indicate that 12.9 million households headed by persons aged 60 or older had a retirement account of some kind at year-end 2005, and that 4.6 million of these households (36%) had account balances of $100,000 or more.

61 "United States Life Tables, 2004," *National Vital Statistics Reports*, vol. 56(9), (December 2007).

62 As an example, consider a man age 85 with $25,000 in an account that loses 10% in value each year for three consecutive years. At age 85, he withdraws 1/7.2 (13.9%) of $25,000, or $3,468. One year later, he withdraws 1/6.8 (14.8%) of $19,379 or $2,864. The next year, he withdraws 1/6.3 (15.8%) of $14,864 or $2,343. The following year he withdraws 1/5.9 (16.9%) of $11,269 or $1,896. If the account earns a positive rate of return, the withdrawals could increase or decrease in size, depending on the rate of investment return.

63 For easier comparison, the initial balance is assumed to be $100,000 in all cases, although an individual who delays retirement until age 65 or 70 might accumulate a larger balance.

64 Stout and Mitchell, *Financial Services Review*, (2006). Another prominent economist has observed that "retiring employees are ill-equipped to set a sensible drawdown program on

their own, especially in the current volatile environment." See the testimony of Shlomo Benartzi, Ph.D. before the House Committee on Education and Labor on October 22, 2008, at http://edlabor.house.gov/testimony/2008-10-22-ShlomoBenartzi.pdf.

[65] Dus, Maurer, and Mitchell, *Financial Services Review*, (2005).

In: The Role of Savings and Other Issues... ISBN: 978-1-60741-446-9
Editor: Joel K. Harris 

*Chapter 5*

# INDIVIDUAL RETIREMENT ACCOUNTS AND 401(K) PLANS: EARLY WITHDRAWALS AND REQUIRED DISTRIBUTIONS*

*Patrick Purcell*

## SUMMARY

In the interest of encouraging workers to save for retirement, Congress has authorized several kinds of retirement savings plans that qualify for reduced or deferred income taxes. These plans provide a financial incentive for people to save, either by allowing workers and employers to deduct from income the amount they contribute to the plan or to take tax-free distributions from the plan after they retire. This CRS report summarizes the provisions of law that govern the taxes applicable to pre-retirement distributions from retirement accounts, and the situations in which distributions must be taken from a plan in order to avoid a tax penalty.

Because tax-deductible contributions to retirement plans and deferral of taxes on investment earnings reduce federal income tax collections, Congress has placed limits on the amount that can be contributed to these plans each year. To assure that the tax preferences granted to retirement accounts are used

* This is an edited, reformatted and augmented version of a CRS Report for Congress publication dated December 2008.

to promote retirement income security rather than to subsidize transfers of wealth from one generation to the next, federal law requires owners of retirement accounts that are funded with tax-deductible contributions to begin taking required minimum distributions from the accounts after they reach age 701/2. Failure to take a required minimum distribution will result in a tax penalty equal to 50% of the amount that should have been distributed. Retirement plans that are funded with after-tax income—like the "Roth IRA"—do not have required minimum distributions during the account owner's lifetime.

To discourage individuals from taking pre-retirement withdrawals from retirement savings accounts, the Internal Revenue Code (I.R.C.) imposes a 10% penalty on withdrawals taken before age 59½, which is levied in addition to any other applicable income tax. Recognizing that some significant events might require people to withdraw money from their retirement accounts earlier than expected, Congress has provided in law for waiving the 10% early withdrawal penalty in some situations. As with required distributions after age 70½, Roth IRAs have a special rule with respect to early withdrawals. Because contributions to a Roth IRA must consist entirely of income on which income tax has already been paid, qualified distributions from a Roth IRA are not subject to income taxes or penalties.

In response to the steep decline in stock prices in 2008, which substantially reduced the value of many retirees' retirement accounts, the House of Representatives on December 10, 2008, passed H.R. 7327, which would suspend for tax year 2009 the required minimum distributions for taxpayers who are over age 70½. On December 12, 2008, H.R. 7327 passed the Senate by unanimous consent. President Bush signed the bill on December 23, 2008.

In the interest of encouraging workers to save for retirement, Congress has authorized the creation of several kinds of retirement savings plans that qualify for reduced or deferred income taxes. These plans provide a financial incentive for people to save, either by allowing workers and employers to deduct from income the amount they contribute to the plans or to take tax-free distributions from the plans after they retire. This CRS report summarizes the provisions of federal law that govern the taxes applicable to pre-retirement distributions from retirement accounts and the situations in which distributions must be taken in order to avoid a tax penalty.

Because tax-deductible contributions to retirement plans and deferral of taxes on investment earnings reduce federal income tax collections, Congress has placed limits on the amount that employers and employees can contribute to these plans each year. As the Government Accountability Office has noted, "these limits exist to prevent partial public subsidies of excessively large retirement benefits through tax preferences."[1] To ensure that the tax preferences granted to retirement accounts are used to promote retirement income security rather than to subsidize transfers of wealth from one generation to the next, Congress has required distributions from retirement accounts that are funded with tax-deductible contributions to begin when the account owner reaches age 70½. A taxpayer who does not take a required minimum distribution is subject to a tax penalty equal to 50% of the amount that should have been distributed. If these distributions were not required, the temporary tax deferrals that Congress has authorized to encourage retirement saving would become permanent tax exemptions for those whose income from other sources is high enough that they do not need to take withdrawals from their retirement savings to help pay their living expenses. Retirement plans that are funded with after-tax income—like the "Roth IRA"—do not have required distributions during the account owner's lifetime.

To discourage individuals from taking pre-retirement withdrawals from retirement savings accounts, the Internal Revenue Code (I.R.C.) imposes a 10% additional tax on withdrawals taken before age 59½. This penalty is levied in addition to regular income taxes. Recognizing that some significant events might require people to withdraw money from their retirement accounts earlier than expected, Congress has provided in law for waiving the 10% early-withdrawal penalty in some situations. As with required minimum distributions, Roth IRAs have a special rule with respect to early withdrawals. Because contributions to a Roth IRA consist entirely of income on which income tax has already been paid, the full amount of Roth IRA contributions can be withdrawn at any time without being subject to additional income taxes or an early withdrawal penalty. Investment earnings on a Roth IRA are free of income taxes and penalties if withdrawn at least five years after the account was established and the account owner has reached age 59½.

## Kinds of Retirement Savings Plans

There are several kinds of retirement savings plans, the most common of which are *individual retirement accounts* (IRAs) and the employer-sponsored plans that are authorized under section 401(k) of the Internal Revenue Code. There are two types of individual retirement account: the "traditional IRA," authorized by Congress in 1974, and the "Roth IRA," which Congress authorized in 1997. The two types of IRA differ in the tax treatment of both contributions and distributions. In a traditional IRA, contributions may be tax-deductible (up to legal limits).

Investment earnings accrue on a tax-deferred basis. Distributions from the plan are taxed as ordinary income.[2] Contributions to a Roth IRA are not tax-deductible; however, qualifying distributions from a Roth IRA are tax-free. The tax treatment of a 401(k) plan is similar to that of a traditional IRA: contributions (up to legal limits) are excluded from income and investment earnings accrue on a tax-deferred basis. Distributions from the plan are taxed as ordinary income. The Economic Growth and Tax Relief Reconciliation Act of 2001 (P.L. 107-16) authorized a "Roth 401(k)" beginning in 2006. Like the Roth IRA, Roth contributions to a 401(k) plan are made on an after-tax basis, and qualified distributions from the plan are tax-free.

## CONTRIBUTION RULES: PUTTING MONEY INTO A RETIREMENT ACCOUNT

### Contribution Rules for Traditional IRAs

In 2008, a worker can make a tax-deductible contribution of $5,000 (or annual earnings, if less) to a traditional IRA if he or she is under age 70½ and neither the worker nor his spouse is covered by an employer-sponsored retirement plan. Workers age 50 and older can make an additional "catch-up" contribution of $1,000. For an unmarried worker who is covered by an employer- sponsored retirement plan, the deduction for tax year 2008 phases out between $53,000 and $63,000 of modified adjusted gross income.[3] For a married worker who is covered by a plan at work, the maximum deductible contribution for tax year 2008 phases out between $85,000 and $105,000 of modified A.G.I. For a married worker who files a joint return and does not have an employer-sponsored retirement plan, but whose spouse is covered by an employer's plan, the maximum deductible contribution phases out between $159,000 and $169,000 of modified A.G.I.

If a traditional IRA has been funded entirely or in part by *after-tax* contributions, the after-tax contributions are deemed by the IRS to be a *pro rata* share of any distribution from the account. The account owner cannot declare all of the distribution to consist entirely of after-tax contributions, and therefore not subject to the income tax. If an individual owns more than one traditional IRA, and any of them have been funded with after-tax contributions, a distribution from *any* of the accounts will be treated as consisting partly of after-tax contributions.

## Contribution Rules for Roth IRAs

The Taxpayer Relief Act of 1997 (P.L. 105-34) authorized a new kind of retirement savings account—the "Roth IRA"—named for former Senator William Roth of Delaware. The distinguishing characteristics of the Roth IRA are that (1) contributions can be made at any age, (2) no distributions from the plan are required during the account owner's lifetime and (3) contributions to the account are not tax-deductible, but qualifying distributions from the account are tax-free. Only individuals whose income is below thresholds defined in law are eligible to contribute to a Roth IRA. For single tax filers, the maximum permissible contribution to a Roth IRA in 2008 phases out for those with modified adjusted gross income between $101,000 and $116,000. For married couples filing jointly, the maximum permissible contribution to a Roth IRA phases out between $159,000 and $169,000 of annual income.[4] For married persons filing separately, the contribution limit phases out between $0 and $10,000 of income. The total annual limit on contributions to all of an individual's IRAs (traditional deductible, traditional nondeductible, and Roth) is $5,000 in 2008 (or $6,000 for individuals age 50 and over). The contribution limit in future years will be indexed to the rate of inflation, as measured by the Consumer Price Index, in $500 increments.

Because all contributions to a Roth IRA are made with after-tax income, the full amount of contributions (the account basis) can be withdrawn tax-free at any time. Distributions from a Roth IRA are deemed to come from contributions first, from "rollovers"second,[5] and account earnings last. Thus, distributions from a Roth IRA are deemed to consist entirely of after-tax contributions until the full amount of those contributions has been withdrawn. This assures that the account owner can withdraw the full amount that he or she has contributed without having to pay additional taxes or early withdrawal penalties on that amount. Distributions from a Roth IRA that exceed the account basis are taxable unless they are *qualified distributions*. These distributions also may be subject to a 10% additional tax if made before age 59½. Distributions that occur after the account owner has reached age 59½ and at least five years after the account was established are qualified distributions. Qualified distributions from a Roth IRA are tax-free.

## Converting a Traditional IRA to a Roth IRA

A traditional IRA can be converted to a Roth IRA, but a Roth IRA cannot be converted to a traditional IRA. Until 2010, only taxpayers with A.G.I. of $100,000 or less (except those who are married and filing separately) can convert a traditional IRA to a Roth IRA.[6] The immediate consequence of converting a traditional IRA to a Roth IRA is that income tax must be paid on the entire amount that is converted, except for any amount that represents after-tax contributions. Any amount that is subject to income tax when a traditional IRA is converted to a Roth IRA must remain in the Roth IRA for at least five years—or until the account owner reaches age 59½, if earlier—or it will be subject to the 10% additional tax on early distributions. If a distribution occurs less than five years after the conversion, the amount that was taxable in the year of the conversion will be subject to the 10% early withdrawal penalty unless the account owner has reached age 59½.[7]

## Contribution Rules for Employer-Sponsored Plans

Under section 401 of the Internal Revenue Code, employers can establish retirement plans that qualify for beneficial tax treatment, including a tax deduction for employer contributions and deferral of income taxes on employee contributions and investment earnings. Section 401(k) allows employers to establish plans in which employees can choose to take their compensation in cash or to defer part of it in the form of a contribution to a retirement plan—called an "elective deferral." These plans—popularly known as 401(k) plans—are referred to in the tax code as "cash or deferred arrangements." Non-profit educational and cultural organizations can offer similar retirement plans under I.R.C. §403(b). State and local governments and tax-exempt organizations can offer deferred compensation arrangements under I.R.C. §457. Although the plans authorized under I.R.C. §401(k), §403(b), and §457 differ from each other in some respects, effective with the Economic Growth and Tax Relief Reconciliation Act of 2001 (EGTRRA, P.L. 107-16), balances in one type of plan generally can be rolled over into either of the others, or into an IRA.

The maximum permissible employee salary deferral under a 401(k) plan in 2008 is the lesser of $15,500 or 100% of compensation.[8] Under the terms of the Economic Growth and Tax Relief Reconciliation Act, the maximum deferral in years after 2006 is indexed to inflation. The maximum salary deferral in 2009 will be $16,500. Participants aged 50 or over can make additional "catch-up" deferrals of up to $5,000 in 2008. The maximum annual addition to a defined contribution plan—the sum of employer and employee contributions—is the lesser of $46,000 or 100% of compensation in 2008.[9] This limit is indexed to the Consumer Price Index (CPI) in $1,000 increments. The annual contribution limits and the minimum distribution rules for §403(b) plans are the same as for 401(k) plans. Since January 1, 2006, participants in 401(k) and 403(b) plans have been permitted to elect "Roth" treatment for their contributions, if their plan chooses to permit them to do so. Such contributions are made on an after-tax basis, but qualified distributions from the account are tax-free. There is no required minimum distribution from a Roth 401(k) during the employee's lifetime or that of the employee's spouse, but any beneficiary other than the account owner's spouse is subject to required minimum distributions.

State and local governments and tax-exempt organizations can establish deferred compensation arrangements under I.R.C. §457.[10] Participants' contributions to these plans are excluded from income, and plan earnings are tax-deferred until withdrawal. The maximum permissible contribution to a §457 plan is the lesser of 100% of compensation or $15,500 in 2008.[11] Participants in §457 plans can make additional contributions of up to twice the standard amount in the last three years before normal retirement age. Participants who are 50 or older can make additional "catch-up" contributions of up to $5,000 in 2008. The EGTRRA of 2001 repealed the rules that coordinated the maximum annual employee contribution to a §457 plan with the contribution limits for other types of plans. Consequently, an employee who participates in a §457 plan and who also participates in either a §403(b) or a §401(k) plan is permitted to contribute up to $15,500 to each plan in 2008. Section 457 plans also are subject to a special rule with respect to distributions. These plans are not subject to the 10% penalty for withdrawals before age 59½, provided that the withdrawal occurs upon retirement or termination of employment.

# DISTRIBUTION RULES: WITHDRAWING MONEYFROM A RETIREMENT ACCOUNT

## Additional Tax on Early Distributions

Section 72(t) of the Internal Revenue Code applies a tax equal to 10% of the amount distributed from a "qualified retirement plan."[12] The 10% additional tax is levied in addition to regular income taxes *unless* the distribution from the retirement plan is madc

(1) after the plan participant has reached age 59½;
(2) to a beneficiary after the death of the participant;
(3) because the participant has become disabled;
(4) to an alternate payee under a qualified domestic relations order (QDRO);[13]
(5) to an employee who has separated from service under an early retirement arrangement after reaching age 55;[14]
(6) as dividends paid from an Employee Stock Ownership Plan (ESOP);
(7) through an IRS levy to collect back taxes owed by the plan participant;
(8) to pay medical expenses of the plan participant, a spouse, or dependent, but only to the extent that they exceed 7.5% of adjusted gross income; or
(9) as part of a series of *substantially equal periodic payments* (SEPPs) over the life of the participant or the joint lives of the participant and a designated beneficiary.

## Special Rules for Traditional IRAs

Two of the exceptions to the 10% penalty apply *only* to employer-sponsored plans, and not to individual retirement accounts. These are distributions to an alternate payee under a QDRO and distributions to a worker who has retired after reaching age 55 but before age 59½. There are, however, three additional exceptions to the 10% early withdrawal penalty that apply *only* to IRAs. Distributions from an individual retirement account made before age 591/2 are not subject to the 10% early withdrawal penalty if the distributions are used

- to pay health insurance premiums during a period of unemployment;
- to pay for qualifying post-secondary educational expenses; or
- to pay up to $10,000 of the cost of purchasing a first home.

There are restrictions on each of these three exceptions. The exception for paying health insurance premiums applies only if the account owner (1) has received unemployment compensation for at least 12 consecutive weeks, (2) receives the distribution either in the same year that unemployment compensation was received or in the following year, and (3) receives the distribution no later than 60 days after returning to work.

The exception for higher-education expenses applies to either the account owner or the account owner's spouse, child, or grandchild, but only if (1) the distribution is used to pay for tuition, fees, books, supplies, equipment, or room and board, and (2) the distribution is no greater than the sum of eligible expenses, minus the amount of any tax-free assistance or scholarships that the student receives, excluding loans, gifts, or inheritances.

For purposes of the exception to the 10% early withdrawal penalty, a "first-time home buyer" is defined as someone who did not own (and whose spouse did not own) a principal residence in the two years preceding the distribution from the account. The exception for a first-home purchase has a lifetime limit of $10,000. The distribution must be used to purchase, build, or re-build the principal residence of the account owner, the account owner's spouse, or the parent or grandparent, or the child or grandchild of the account owner or the account owner's spouse. In addition, the distribution must be used within 120 days or else rolled over into another IRA.

## Early Withdrawals Without Penalty: "Substantially Equal Periodic Payments"

Section 72(t) of the Internal Revenue Code states that, if distributions from a qualified retirement plan made before age 59½ are "part of a series of substantially equal periodic payments," they are not subject to the 10% penalty that otherwise would apply.[15] Under this exception to the 10% early withdrawal penalty, an account owner can begin taking distributions from a retirement plan at any age; however, these distributions can be taken only from a plan sponsored by a former employer or from an IRA. The distributions also

(1) must be paid at least once each year;
(2) must be based on the life expectancy of the plan participant or the joint life expectancy of the participant and a designated beneficiary; and
(3) must not be modified before the *later of* five years after the first distribution or the date on which the plan participant reaches age 59½.

The Internal Revenue Service has defined in regulation the forms of distribution that it will consider to be "substantially equal periodic payments" and therefore will not be subject to the 10% tax penalty otherwise applicable to early withdrawals.[16] The IRS has approved three methods for calculating substantially equal periodic payments. They are

- the *minimum distribution method,* also called the life expectancy method;
- the *amortization method,* which amortizes an account balance using life expectancy tables and a "reasonable" interest rate; and
- the *annuitization method*, which divides the account balance by an annuity factor based on a "reasonable" mortality table and interest rate.

For any individual, each of the three methods may produce a different distribution amount. As its name implies, the *minimum distribution method* will usually result in the smallest annual distribution. It is also the only one of the three methods in which the amount of the distribution is likely to vary from year to year. The distribution amount varies both because of changes in the remaining account balance and changes in the account owner's remaining life expectancy. The amortization method and the annuitization method usually produce distributions that are similar in size because the same economic and demographic variables determine the distribution amounts under both of these methods. The distribution amount is calculated *annually* under the minimum distribution method. Under the amortization and annuitization methods, this calculation is typically performed only before the first distribution and the distribution remains unchanged from year to year.

One way to receive a larger annual distribution than would result from the minimum distribution method, but smaller than the distribution produced by either of the other two methods, is to "segment" one's retirement accounts into two or more IRAs. Distributions can then be taken from one (or more) of them while leaving the others intact. According to one authoritative source, "IRS rulings have consistently allowed taxpayers to take periodic payments from one or more plans and not others."[17]

### *The Minimum Distribution Method*

Under the minimum distribution method, the annual distribution in any year is determined by dividing the account balance for that year by the account owner's remaining life expectancy, (or the joint life expectancy of the account owner and his or her designated beneficiary) as published in a life expectancy table that has been approved by the IRS. Because the account balance and the account owner's remaining life expectancy change from year to year, the distribution amount also will change each year under this method.

Although the amount of the distribution will change each year under the minimum distribution method, the IRS treats the resulting distributions as substantially equal periodic payments for purposes of section 72(t). Once the distributions have begun, however, the account owner may neither stop receiving payments nor switch to one of the other two methods until *the later of* (1) five years after the first distribution or (2) the date on which the plan participant reaches age 59½. Terminating or altering the distributions before the later of these two dates will result in a penalty of 10% (plus interest) being levied retroactively on all distributions that have been made from the plan.

### *The Amortization Method*

Under the amortization method, the amount of the annual distribution is based on the account owner's remaining life expectancy in the year of the first distribution and a "reasonable" rate of interest. (If the account owner has a designated beneficiary, the distribution is based on their joint life expectancies in the year of the first distribution.) Under this method, the account balance and remaining life expectancy are determined only for the first distribution year. The annual distribution is the same amount in each succeeding year. The risk to the account owner who chooses the amortization method is that a declining account balance might result in the account being exhausted in fewer years than he or she had expected when the distributions began.

### *The Annuitization Method*

Under the annuitization method, the distribution amount is determined by dividing the account balance by an *annuity factor*. This factor represents the present value[18] of an annuity of $1 per year beginning at the taxpayer's current age and continuing for the life of the account owner (or the joint lives of the account owner and a designated beneficiary). The annuity factor must be derived from life expectancy tables published by the Internal Revenue Service and an interest rate that does not exceed 120% of the federal mid-term rate.[19] Under this method, the account balance, the annuity factor, and the interest rate are determined only once, for the first distribution year. The resulting annual payment is the same amount in each succeeding year. In private letter rulings, the IRS generally has allowed the distribution amount to be adjusted annually to account for changes in life expectancy and account balance. The IRS also has issued private letter rulings that allow the annual distribution to be increased for inflation. A private letter ruling, however, applies *only* to the individual who requested it. These rulings cannot be relied upon by other taxpayers as legally binding statements of IRS policy.

***Examples***

Consider a 55-year-old unmarried individual with no designated beneficiary who began taking substantially equal periodic payments in October 2008. The two relevant variables for determining the distribution amount under the *minimum distribution method* are the account balance and the account owner's remaining life expectancy, which for a 55-year-old is 29.6 years.[20] If we assume an account balance of $100,000 on September 30, 2008, the first-year distribution would be *$3,378*, which is derived by dividing the account balance by the individual's remaining life expectancy. In each succeeding year, the annual distribution amount would be determined by the same process—dividing the remaining account balance (which may have increased or decreased depending on investment returns) by the individual's remaining life expectancy, which will decrease each year. Because the minimum distribution method takes into account changes in both the account balance and remaining life expectancy, the annual distribution amount will change from year to year under this method.

Under the *amortization method*, the annual distribution for an individual in the circumstances described above would be *$5,824*.[21] The annual distribution under this method is determined the same way that a loan repayment is calculated. The account balance is analogous to the principal of the loan, the term is the person's remaining life expectancy in the year that the first distribution is made, and the interest rate is equal to or less than 120% of the mid-term federal interest rate in either of the two months immediately preceding the first distribution. Under the amortization method, the amount of the annual distribution is determined once, before the first distribution, and it remains the same from year to year.

Under the *annuitization method*, the annual distribution for an individual in the circumstances described above also would be *$5,824.*[22] The variables that determine the annual distribution under the annuitization method are, as under the amortization method, the individual's remaining life expectancy and an interest rate. As a result, the distribution amounts under these two methods are likely to be nearly the same, provided that similar interest rates are used. The distribution amount is easier to compute under the annuitization method because the interest rate and life expectancy factors have been combined into a single number called an *annuity factor*. There is a single annuity factor for each possible combination of interest rate and term (life expectancy). These factors are readily available in published sources such as *McGraw-Hill's Compound Interest Annuity Tables* and *Archer's Compound Interest and Annuity Tables*. To find the annual distribution amount, the account balance is simply divided by the annuity factor appropriate to the individual's age and the applicable rate of interest.

## Revenue Ruling 2002-62

Both the amortization method and the annuitization method of calculating substantially equal periodic payments result in distribution amounts that are constant from year to year and that are larger than the initial distribution that results from the minimum distribution method. In October 2002, the Internal Revenue Service released Revenue Ruling 2002-62, which allows taxpayers to make a one-time switch from either the amortization method or the annuitization method to the minimum distribution method of calculating the annual distribution from their retirement plans. The smaller distributions that result from this switch will prevent retirement accounts from being depleted as rapidly as would occur under either of the other two methods.

Revenue ruling 2002-62 also states that

- If an account owner takes periodic payments (SEPPs) and his or her account is exhausted before age 59½, the IRS will not treat this as a "modification" of the method of distribution and will not assess the

10% penalty and retroactive interest changes that otherwise would be levied.

- An interest rate of up to 120% of the federal mid-term rate for either of the two months immediately preceding the month in which the distribution begins can be used under either the amortization or annuity methods.
- A distribution can be based on the account balance on December 31 of the previous year or any date in the current year prior to the first distribution. In subsequent years, under the minimum distribution method, the distribution can be based on the value either on December 31 of the prior year or on a date within a reasonable period before that year's distribution.
- Distributions can be based on any one of the three life expectancy tables published by the IRS in Publication 590. (The *Single Life Expectancy* table yields the highest annual distribution). Also, a new mortality table for the annuity method, published in Appendix B of Revenue Ruling 2002-62, must be used for SEPPs starting on or after January 1, 2003. The new tables reflect increases in life expectancy and decreasing mortality.

## REQUIRED MINIMUM DISTRIBUTIONS

In order to encourage employers to sponsor retirement plans and employees to participate in these plans, Congress has amended the Internal Revenue Code to (1) allow employer contributions to qualified retirement plans to be treated as tax-deductible business expenses, (2) exclude employer contributions to retirement plans and investment earnings on those plans from employee income, and (3) permit qualifying employee contributions to individual retirement accounts and certain employer-sponsored plans to be excluded from taxable income in the year the contribution is made and to exclude investment earnings on these contributions from annual income. These contributions and investment earnings are taxed when the retirement account is distributed to the plan participant, usually during retirement.

To ensure that tax-deferred retirement accounts that have been established to provide income during retirement are not used as permanent tax shelters or as vehicles for transmitting wealth to heirs, Congress has required plan participants to begin taking distributions from these plans no later than April 1 of the year after they reach age 70½.[23] Participants in employer-sponsored plans who are still working at age 70½ can delay distributions until April 1 of the year after they have retired. This exception does not apply to traditional IRAs.[24] In a traditional IRA, the required beginning date for distributions is always April 1 of the year after the participant reaches age 70½. The distributions must be made over the life expectancy of the plan participant, or over the joint life expectancy of the plan participant and his or her designated beneficiary. Failure to take a required distribution will result in a tax penalty equal to 50% of the amount that should have been distributed.[25]

The tax code requires that either the entire retirement account balance must be distributed by the required beginning date, or that distributions must have begun by that date with the amount of the distributions based on the remaining life expectancy of the account owner (or the joint life expectancy of the account owner and a designated beneficiary.)[26] For most participants in employer-sponsored plans, the "required beginning date" for distributions is April 1 of the calendar year following the *later of* (1) the year in which the plan participant reaches age 70½, or (2) the year in which he or she retires.[27] If the plan participant owns 5% or more of the company, however, the required beginning date is always April 1 of the year after the participant reaches age 70½, regardless of whether he or she has retired.

If required minimum distributions have begun but the account owner dies before the entire account balance has been distributed, the remainder of the account must be distributed at least as rapidly as under the distribution method that was being used when the account owner died. The account must then be distributed over the remaining life expectancy of the designated beneficiary, or if there is no designated beneficiary, over a length of time equal to the remaining life expectancy of the decedent in the year of his or her death.

If an account owner dies before the required distributions from the account have begun and no beneficiary has been designated, the entire account balance must be distributed within five years after the death of the account owner. Any amount that is to be paid to a designated beneficiary can be distributed over his or her life expectancy, provided that the distributions begin no later than one year after the date of the account owner's death. If the designated beneficiary is the surviving spouse of the account owner, then the required beginning date for distributions is the date on which the account owner would have reached age 70½.[28] The account balance for determining the amount of the required distribution each year is the balance on the last valuation date in the year preceding the distribution.[29] In most cases, this will be December 31. A surviving spouse who is the sole designated beneficiary also has the option to roll over the account into an IRA in his or her own name. In that case, the surviving spouse generally will have to wait until age 59½ to begin taking distributions, just as if the IRA had always been in the surviving spouse's name.

Section 634 of the Economic Growth and Tax Relief Reconciliation Act of 2001 (P.L. 107-16) directed the Secretary of the Treasury to modify the life expectancy tables under the regulations relating to required minimum distributions so that the tables reflect current life expectancy. The IRS issued the required regulations on April 17, 2002.[30] The new regulations incorporate life tables that reflect increases in life expectancy since the 1980s, when the tables were last published. Consequently, the minimum required annual distribution is smaller than under the old life tables, because an account balance now will be distributed over a longer expected life span.

Required distributions do not compel account owners to sell the stocks, bonds, or other assets in which a retirement account is invested. The law requires funds to be withdrawn from the retirement account and income taxes paid on the amount withdrawn, but this requirement this does not require assets to be sold. Stocks, for example, can be transferred from an IRA to a regular brokerage account. If assets that have been transferred from a retirement account to a regular account later increase in value, the increase will be taxed as capital gains, which are taxed at lower rates than ordinary income. If the age at which distributions are required were to be pushed beyond age 70½, future distributions would probably be larger because required distributions are based on both the account value and the account owner's remaining life expectancy. For any given account balance, a required distribution beginning at age 75, for example, would be greater than a distribution beginning at age 71, because the account owner will have a shorter remaining life expectancy. Larger annual distributions could push some retirees into higher tax brackets.

Eliminating required distributions altogether would, of course, provide account owners with the maximum freedom of choice about when to take distributions from their accounts.[31] The accounts eventually would be subject to taxation because, under current law the designated beneficiary usually is required to take withdrawals over his or her life expectancy. Some accounts also might be subject to the estate tax. In fact, however, extending the tax deferral period would benefit only those account owners whose income from other sources is sufficient to allow them to postpone withdrawals from their retirement accounts. Retirees who need to take distributions from their retirement accounts to supplement their retirement income, rather than because they are required by law to do so, would not benefit from delaying or eliminating the beginning date for required distributions. Lower and middle-income retirees who need to take distributions to support themselves in retirement would still have to take distributions from their accounts and pay income taxes on those distributions if their income is above the threshold for taxation.

One of the attractions of the Roth IRA is that no distributions are required from these plans during the account owner's lifetime. After the Roth IRA was authorized by Congress in 1997, many owners of traditional IRAs converted their accounts to Roth IRAs and paid income tax on the amounts that they converted. Some of those who converted their traditional IRAs to Roth IRAs might be unhappy if Congress were to eliminate required distributions from traditional IRAs. This would grant to current IRA owners free of charge a benefit that others purchased by converting their traditional IRAs to Roth IRAs and paying income taxes on the converted amounts.

## How Many People Are Subject to RMDs?

Required minimum distributions from a traditional IRA or from a 401(k) account owned by a retired worker must begin no later than April of the year after the account owner reaches age 70½. In 2005, an estimated 16.9 million households were headed by persons aged 70 and older, and 5.5 million (32.5%) of these households owned at least one IRA or 401(k)-type retirement account. Of the 5.5 million households potentially subject to required minimum distributions in 2005, 2.9 million (53%) had retirement account balances of less than $50,000 and 938,000 (17%) had balances of more than $200,000. (See **Table 1**.) Almost 3.6 million (65%) of the households potentially subject to RMDs had total income of less than $50,000 in 2005, while 415,000 households (7.6%) had total income of more than $100,000.

## One-Year Moratorium on RMDs in 2009

Individuals who fail to take required distributions from a retirement account are subject to a tax penalty equal to 50% of the required distribution. On December 10, the House of Representatives passed H.R. 7327, which would suspend the 50% tax for failure to take a required minimum distribution in 2009.[32] On December 12, 2008, H.R. 7327 passed the Senate by unanimous consent. President Bush signed the bill on December 23, 2008.[33]

**Table 1. Number of Households Headed by Persons Age 70 or Older with an IRA or 401(k) Account in 2005 (number of households, in thousands)**

| Total Household Retirement Account Balance | | | | | |
|---|---|---|---|---|---|
| | **Under $50,000** | **$50,000 to $99,999** | **$100,000 to $199,999** | **$200,000 or more** | **Total** |
| **Age of Householder** | | | | | |
| 70 to 79 | 1,992 | 667 | 597 | 715 | 3,971 |
| 80 or older | 915 | 245 | 140 | 223 | 1,524 |
| **Household Income** | | | | | |
| Under $50,000 | 2,074 | 633 | 345 | 534 | 3,586 |
| $50,000-$99,999 | 699 | 225 | 279 | 291 | 1,494 |
| $100,000 or more | 135 | 54 | 114 | 112 | 415 |
| **Total** | **2,908** | **912** | **737** | **938** | **5,495** |

Source: Bureau of the Census, Survey of Income and Program Participation.

Notes: Total household retirement account balance is the sum of all individual retirement account balances and defined contribution plan balances of all members of the household.

## Plan Loans

The Internal Revenue Code allows participants in employer-sponsored plans to borrow from their accounts, but plans are not required to allow such loans. A loan cannot exceed the greater of $10,000 or 50% of the participant's vested account balance. In no case may it exceed $50,000. A loan from a retirement plan must be paid back within five years at a "reasonable" rate of interest. If repayment ceases, the IRS will treat the full amount of the loan as a distribution from the plan, and it will be subject to income tax and possibly to an early distribution penalty. If the employee separates from the employer before the loan is repaid, the full amount must be repaid, or it will be treated as a distribution from the plan.[34]

## HARDSHIP DISTRIBUTIONS

The tax code permits 401(k) plans—and no other kind of tax-qualified retirement plan—to make distributions available "upon hardship of the employee."[35] Although the I.R.C. allows plans to make these distributions available, it does not require them to do so. Federal regulations specify that a hardship distribution can be made only on account of "an immediate and heavy financial need of the employee" and cannot exceed the amount of the employee's previous elective contributions.[36] Qualifying expenses include medical care for the participant and/or family members, the purchase of a principal residence, college tuition and related expenses, expenses to prevent eviction or foreclosure on a principal residence, and funeral expenses. The distribution must be limited to the amount needed to meet the employee's immediate financial need plus any taxes that will result from the distribution. Employees are prohibited by law from making contributions to a plan for a period of six months after a hardship distribution. Hardship distributions are always subject to ordinary income taxes, but if the distribution is used for a purpose specifically designated in IRC section 72(t) the distribution will not be subject to the 10% early withdrawal penalty, even if the plan participant is under age 59½.[37]

## ROTH IRA DISTRIBUTIONS

Distributions of investment earnings from a Roth IRA are subject to regular income taxes and early withdrawal penalties unless they are *qualified distributions*. Qualified distributions are those that occur after age 59½ and more than five years after the account was established. Investment earnings withdrawn from a Roth IRA before age 59½ are subject to both regular income taxes and a 10% early-withdrawal penalty. Distributions of investment earnings after age 59½ are not subject to the early withdrawal penalty, but they are subject to regular income tax if the distribution occurs less than five years after the account was established. Unlike a traditional IRA, from which required minimum distributions must begin no later than April 1 of the year after the account owner reaches age 70½, there is no requirement for an account owner to take distributions from a Roth IRA at any time during his or her lifetime.

## End Notes

[1] *Private Pensions: Issues of Coverage and Increasing Contribution Limits for Defined Contribution Plans*, GAO-01- 846, September 2001, p. 1.

[2] Income is classified as either "ordinary income" or "capital gains." For tax year 2008, the top marginal tax rate on ordinary income is 35%. The tax rate on capital gains is 15%.

[3] Modified AGI is adjusted gross income plus income from education savings bonds, interest paid on education loans, employer-provided adoption assistance benefits, IRA deductions, deductions for qualified higher education expenses, and some other adjustments.

[4] The income limit for converting a traditional IRA to a Roth IRA is lower. In tax years before 2010, if modified adjusted gross income (AGI) exceeds $100,000 for either a single filer or a married couple, then a traditional IRA cannot be converted to a Roth IRA.

[5] A "rollover" is a deposit that came directly from another tax-qualified retirement account.

[6] P.L. 109-222 (May 16, 2006) repealed the $100,000 income limit for converting a traditional IRA to a Roth IRA beginning in 2010.

[7] Distributions that occur after five years have passed and after age 59½ are "qualified distributions" and are not subject to either ordinary income taxes or tax penalties.

[8] 26 U.S.C. §402(g).

[9] 26 U.S.C. §415(c). The maximum annual addition to a DC plan in 2009 will be $49,000.

[10] Tax-exempt organizations are described in I.R.C. §501(c)(3).

[11] 26 U.S.C. §457(e).

[12] A qualified retirement plan is defined in statute at 26 U.S.C. §4974(c) as "(1) a plan described in section 401(a) which includes a trust exempt from tax under section 501(a), (2) an annuity plan described in section 403(a), (3) an annuity contract described in section 403(b), (4) an individual retirement account described in section 408(a), or (5) an individual retirement annuity described in section 408(b)."

[13] A Qualified Domestic Relations Order divides the assets of a couple at divorce. The alternate payee is usually a former spouse and/or a minor dependent of the divorced couple.

[14] The individual is not prohibited from being employed, or even from returning to work for the same employer, but there must be a period of separation that began after age 55.

[15] 26 U.S.C. §72(t)(2)(A)(iv).

[16] I.R.S. Notice 89-25 (March 20, 1989) and Revenue Ruling 2002-62 (October 3, 2002).

[17] Twila Slesnick and John C. Suttle, *IRAs, 401(k)s, and Other Retirement Plans: Taking Your Money Out*, Fourth Edition, (2002), page 4/4.

[18] A present value is the lump-sum equivalent of a series of payments or stream of income. Present value depends mainly on the length of time over which the money will be paid and the rate of interest at which these payments will be discounted to the present.

[19] The current federal mid-term rate can be found on the IRS website at http://www.irs.gov/taxpros/lists/0,,id= 98042,00.html.

[20] IRS Publication 590, Appendix C, Table 1. *In Arizona Governing Commission for Tax Deferred Annuity & Deferred Compensation Plans v. Norris*, 463 U.S. 1073 (1983), the Supreme Court held that an employer-sponsored plan using sex-segregated life expectancy tables to calculate annuity payments had violated Title VII of the Civil Rights Act of 1964. As a result of this decision, annuities paid from employer sponsored retirement plans must use "unisex" life tables. The ruling does not apply to individually purchased annuities, which may use gender-specific life tables.

[21] Amount is based on an interest rate of 4.0% and a remaining life expectancy of 29.6 years.

[22] This is based on an annuity factor of 17.1687. See http://www.studyfinance.com/common/table4.pdf for the annuity factors used.

[23] 26 U.S.C. §401(a)(9).

[24] Distributions are not required from a Roth IRA during the account owner's lifetime.

[25] 26 U.S.C. §4974.

[26] Life expectancy may be redetermined annually. (See 26 U.S.C. §401(a)(9)(D)).

[27] If a plan participant retires after reaching age 70½, the employee's accrued benefit must be actuarially increased to take into account the period after age 701/2 in which the employee was not receiving any benefits under the plan. (See 26 U.S.C. §401(a)(9)(C)(iii)).

[28] Any distribution required under an incidental death benefit requirement is treated as a required minimum distribution.

[29] 26 C.F.R. §1.401(a)(9)-5, published in the *Federal Register*, vol. 67 no. 4, April 17 , 2002.

[30] *Federal Register*, vol. 67 no. 74, April 17, 2002, pages 18988 to 19028.

[31] Roth IRAs have no minimum distribution requirement during the account owner's lifetime. Roth IRAs are funded only with contributions on which income taxes have already been paid. The investment earnings of a Roth IRA are available tax-free in retirement.

[32] Section 201 of H.R. 7327 provides that distribution under Internal Revenue Code §401(a)(9) will not be required in 2009. The temporary suspension of RMDs applies to all retirement plans under IRC §401 and §403, to plans under §457 maintained by units of state and local governments, and to individual retirement accounts.

[33] "Bush to Sign Pension Funding Relief Bill, White House Spokesman Says," *Daily Tax Report*, BNA, December 18, 2008.

[34] Loans are not permitted from IRAs, but money in an IRA can, in effect, be "borrowed" for 60 days because the law states that any distribution from an IRA that is not deposited in the same or another IRA within 60 days is a taxable distribution. (26 U.S.C. § 408(d)).

[35] 26 U.S.C. §401(k)(2)(B)(i)(IV). It is not necessary for the tax code to include a provision allowing hardship distributions from an IRA because a participant can always withdraw money from an IRA. Such distributions are always taxable, except any portion that is attributable to after-tax contributions. I.R.C. §72(t) describes the kinds of distributions made before age 59½ that are exempt from the 10% additional tax on early distributions.

[36] 26 C.F.R. §1.401(k)-1(d).

[37] Although the I.R.C. allows distributions to be made without penalty beginning at age 59½, many employer plans allow distributions only after the employee has left the employer.

In: The Role of Savings and Other Issues… ISBN: 978-1-60741-446-9
Editor: Joel K. Harris 

*Chapter 6*

# BEHAVIORAL FINANCE, THE MARKET CRISIS AND RETIREMENT SAVINGS*

***Shlomo Benartzi****

Thank you Chairman Miller and members of the House Committee on Education and Labor for the opportunity to share with you my views on behavioral finance, the market crisis and retirement savings.

My name is Shlomo Benartzi. I am a Professor and co-chair of the Behavioral Decision Making Group at the Anderson School of Management at UCLA. I am also co-founder of the Behavioral Finance Forum (BeFi). I have spent the last 15 years researching participant behavior in 401(k) plans, with a particular focus on using behavioral economics to increase retirement savings and retirement security. Some of you might be familiar with the automatic savings increase program Richard Thaler of the University of Chicago and I designed about a decade ago, which we dubbed Save More Tomorrow (or SMarT).

Let me begin my testimony by outlining the behavioral principles that guide retirement savers and how these behavioral tendencies could undermine the retirement security of 401(k) participants in the current environment. To keep this chapter brief, let me focus on just three behavioral principles that could weaken retirement security.

---

* This is an edited, reformatted and augmented version of a House Education and Labor Committee presentation on October 22, 2008.

1. *Buy High, Sell Low:* Individuals have a tendency to buy at the peak, and then panic when markets drop and sell at the bottom. We saw this happen with the Internet bubble when individuals bought a lot of technology stocks at the end of 1999 and the beginning of 2000 right before the market crashed. We also saw individuals pulling money out of the stock market in 2002 right before the market started to go up. There is a real concern that individuals will repeat the same mistake during this market crisis and sell at the bottom and perhaps even stop contributing to their retirement plan.

2. *Myopic Loss Aversion:* The term "myopic loss aversion" refers to the tendency of individuals to focus on short-term losses, even if they have 20 or 30 years until retirement. The myopic focus on short - term losses could result in individuals chasing safety and placing all their retirement savings in cash. And, we know that a portfolio invested 100 percent in cash is unlikely to provide the long - term growth that many individuals need to fund their retirement. The unusual market volatility we have experienced over the past few weeks and months could magnify the degree of myopia and loss aversion individuals display.

3. *Excessive extrapolation:* Individual investors tend to place too much weight on past performance. For example, many buy stock funds after they see a few years of positive returns. Similarly, the propensity of employees to invest in company stock is highly correlated with the past performance of company stock. I suspect that a lot of employees who were chasing performance and invested heavily in company stock a couple of years ago have recently suffered major losses. This probably includes many employees of financial institutions who invested in company stock and lost their savings and jobs at the same time. Interestingly, preliminary data on recent activity in 401(k) plans indicates that the average participant moved money into company stock in September and early October, probably misjudging the risk of company stock.

The three behavioral principles outlined above highlight the risk of individuals mismanaging their retirement savings, especially in the current economic environment. And, I do believe some retirement savers will panic and bail out of the stock market at the wrong time. I also believe, however, that inertia is extremely powerful and a lot of individuals are likely to procrastinate and never take any action. In the current environment, sticking to one's longterm plans and avoiding impulsive actions might actually be the best decision, even if it is caused by inertia and procrastination.

Having highlighted "behavioral obstacles" that tend to undermine the retirement security of many people, the real question is what can be done to help employees better plan for retirement? I believe Congress has already made significant contributions to the retirement security of Americans with the Pension Protection Act. In particular, automatic enrollment and automatic increases made saving for retirement a lot easier for many Americans. Similarly, clarifying what constitutes a Qualified Default Investment Alternative made plan sponsors more comfortable choosing balanced portfolios on behalf of their plan participants, rather than playing it safe with the most conservative option. However, our system should be improved to help individuals better plan for retirement. Below I list three key areas that I believe could be improved.

1. *Participant Information:*

   a. *Highlight Long Term Performance on First Page of Statements:* Defined contribution plans are required to provide quarterly statements. Unfortunately, a lot of plan providers interpret that requirement as having to highlight the most recent quarter's performance on the first page of the statement. Since individuals are already obsessed with short term performance, why not use the quarterly statements as an opportunity to promote long term thinking? In particular, I propose that the statements display longer term results on the first page, then provide the recent quarter numbers on the second (or last) page. While this might be permissible under the current law, an endorsement of the idea might be all that is needed to get plan providers to design more sensible participant communications.

   b. *Provide Retirement Income Projections on Statements:* I argue that most individuals are ill-equipped to analyze rates of return. The goal of a retirement plan is to provide retirement income, so why not translate account balances, deferral rates and investment elections into projected retirement income? Such projections would not be exact, but they would certainly be more informative for the average plan participant. And, they would dampen the effects of volatile financial markets, as they would incorporate both existing balances and future contributions. For example, someone who just experienced a 40 percent decline in his/her account balance might notice just a 10 percent decline in his projected retirement income once future contributions are taken into account. Again, an endorsement might be all that is needed to get plan providers to add income projections to quarterly statements.

2. *Company Stock:*

   a. *Stop the Preferential Treatment of Company Stock:* Company stock enjoys special treatment under ERISA, exempting it from the diversification requirement. It is the only investment option offered to plan participants that is undiversified. I believe, however, that all investments offered to plan participants should be well - diversified, that is, comply with ERISA's diversification requirement. I would like to clarify that I am not proposing to disallow company stock in defined contribution plans. I am just proposing that company stock pass the same fiduciary standards other investments must pass. Of course, if company stock is inherently undiversified and will fail basic fiduciary standards, then plan sponsors will voluntarily stop offering it. I view that as a good thing. We saw thousands of Enron employees lose their jobs and retirement savings simultaneously, and I predict the current crisis will result in many more employees losing their retirement savings due to concentrated positions in company stock.

   b. *Endorse Gradual Diversification Programs:* Many plan sponsors are concerned about the financial security of employees investing in company stock. However, they do not know what to do about it. If they tell employees to diversify and sell the stock, then employees might wrongly believe that the company is in trouble. And, if they offer employees the option to gradually trim down their company stock exposure, they could possibly be liable for selling the stock at the wrong time. Professor Richard Thaler and

I promote the idea of offering employees the option to gradually sell their stock holdings, perhaps keeping a modest amount of say five percent of their savings in company stock. We dubbed our proposed program, "Sell More Tomorrow." Endorsing some type of a gradual diversification program could make plan sponsors more comfortable addressing the company stock problem before it is too late.

3. Retirement Income Solutions:

   a. *Define "Qualified Retirement Income Solutions":* The Pension Protection Act has shed light on best practices for the accumulation stage. In particular, it endorsed automatically enrolling employees into retirement savings plans and automatically escalating their deferral rates overtime. We are already seeing that the mere endorsement of these best practices by Congress resulted in many plan sponsors adopting the proposed changes.

      Unfortunately, the Pension Protection Act did not spell out best practices for the decumulation phase. In particular, it did not provide any guidance on what would constitute appropriate retirement income solutions for employees getting ready to retire. As a result, the vast majority of plan sponsors are totally confused about: (a) whether or not making retirement income solutions available to retiring employees is part of their duties and responsibilities, and (b) what type of retirement income solutions would be prudent to offer. Given that, it is not surprising that most plan sponsors do not offer any retirement income solution through the plan. Retirees are given a lump sum of cash and sent out into their golden years searching for a solution on their own. As we all know, most individuals are illequipped to handle such a complicated financial decision.

      I encourage regulators and legislators to shed light on best practices for the decumulation stage. Again, I believe an endorsement would encourage the industry – both plan sponsors and providers – to create and offer competitive retirement income solutions.

      The current financial crisis also highlights the need to rethink the type of retirement income solutions that would be prudent. For example, is an immediate annuity that pays monthly income for life prudent, given that insurance companies have recently failed to properly manage risks? I do not necessarily have the answers, but I do know that without guidance from regulators and legislators, plan sponsors will not offer any retirement income solutions. And, I do know that retiring employees are ill-equipped to set a sensible drawdown program on their own, especially in the current volatile environment.

b. *Evaluate Longevity Bonds:* Both defined benefit and defined contribution plans face longevity risk, that is, the risk that people will live much longer than was anticipated, leading to the possibility that plan assets will run out. Note that insurance companies do not presently have the financial instruments available to them to manage systematic increases in longevity where most people end up living longer than reserved for. Systematic longevity risk is simply too large for insurance companies to handle. Furthermore, it is not diversifiable internationally, as medical advances in say the US will end up increasing longevity in all countries sooner or later.
The government could help facilitate the creation of a market for hedging systematic longevity risk by issuing longevity bonds. These are bonds that pay more if people live longer and vice versa, and are similar in concept to TIPS (which allow the private sector hedge another systematic risk, namely inflation risk). Not only would longevity bonds enable retirement plans to better manage longevity risk, they would, more importantly, enable insurance companies to better price and guarantee lifetime income streams. This is because longevity bonds would help to establish the market price of longevity risk, in the same way that TIPS help to establish the inflation risk premium. I must admit I am not an expert on launching new markets, but there are experts who have studied these issues extensively. I think establishing a committee to evaluate the merits of longevity bonds is appropriate. Professors David Blake and Robert Shiller would be superb candidates to serve on such a committee.

In summary, improving participant information, addressing the company stock problem and incorporating retirement income solutions into defined contribution plans could enhance the retirement security of millions of people. And, some of the changes I propose could also address behavioral obstacles such as myopic loss aversion and excessive extrapolation.

Keeping in mind the regulatory burden employers already face by offering a retirement plan, my proposals focus on endorsing better practices without necessarily*forcing* or *requiring* plan sponsors and plan providers to implement new or expensive options. To the extent that the proposed changes make sense, I believe mere endorsement by regulators and legislators might be sufficient to make a difference.

Again, thank you Chairman Miller and members of the committee for the opportunity to share my views.

# INDEX

## A



## B



## C

## D



## E



## F



## G

## H



## I



## J



## L



## M

## S



## T



## U



## V



## W